"This workbook comprehensively helps survivors of narcissistic abuse selves the harmful messages they have received from narcissistic tried-and-true dialectical behavior therapy (DBT) techniques from a trauma-informed lens will allow readers to start practicing these skills from the comfort of their own homes. This is a great resource for individuals wanting to delve deeper into healing from narcissistic forms of abuse and gaslighting."

—**Lori Kucharski, PhD, LMFT-S, LPC-S, CEDS-C**, EMDRIA-certified therapist, consultant, and training/credit provider

"Katelyn has written the best workbook I have ever read. In addition to well-researched and ordered content, she writes so that the layperson can easily access and utilize the important concepts in the text, while providing the depth needed for professionals. Her thematic organization and compassionate style encourage readers to become engaged learners as they make their way through the text. This book has the opportunity to change lives."

—**Cindy J. LeMieux, LCSW**, therapist in private practice; DBT-certified and trained in cognitive behavioral therapy (CBT), eye movement desensitization and reprocessing (EMDR), and polyvagal theory; and Reiki master

"Such an affirming and necessary resource for anyone who has experienced narcissistic abuse and gaslighting; with practical insights and clinical tips you can use independently or with a clinical provider. This timely workbook will help you harness the effectiveness of DBT, find healing, and empower you to move forward. Katelyn provides empathic guidance and essential skills you can immediately integrate to claim a renewed sense of self."

—**Melanie Sosinski Brown, LCSW, LADC, CCS**, specializes in navigating developmental trauma and addiction recovery

"Katelyn instills hope that you *can* recover from narcissistic abuse and gaslighting, and provides a clear path forward to reclaiming yourself. This workbook is packed with evidence-based tools that will help you manage your emotions and rebuild your self-worth. The information and exercises in this workbook are a gift to survivors. Our field has needed a book like this for a long time."

> —**Jaime Castillo, LCSW**, founder of Find Your Shine Therapy,
>   and author of *What Happened to Make You Anxious?*

"Baxter-Musser coherently identifies the signs to look for in a narcissistic gaslighting relationship, and provides tangible strategies to heal from them. The included DBT worksheets and self-compassion exercises provide meaningful ways to guide an individual from the dark to a place of health and healing. This is an easy-to-follow manual that may be used as an aid within a therapy session or as a self-help guide."

> —**Stephanie Glitsos, LCSW**, specializes in the treatment of depression,
>   anxiety, post-traumatic stress disorder (PTSD) and borderline personality
>   disorder in the Veteran population

"Katelyn Baxter-Musser is a seasoned therapist who is committed to working with women and those who have experienced abuse. This is the book she was meant to write. It is a comprehensive, clear, and user-friendly guide—full of information, ideas, and exercises to promote the healing process. If an individual has experienced narcissistic abuse, this is the place to begin the healing journey. I will recommend this to many clients."

> —**Nancy J. Abel, LCSW, LADC**, psychotherapist in private practice in
>   South Portland, ME; and coauthor of *Treating Addictions with EMDR*
>   *Therapy and the Stages of Change*

"I highly recommend this workbook for anyone needing skills and support after enduring narcissistic abuse and/or gaslighting from someone in their life. This book is written to be a self-help guide or, better yet, to be used with the guidance of a trained therapist. This workbook does a wonderful job of incorporating the skill of self-compassion, which is crucial for survivors in managing the emotional toll of narcissistic abuse. This book provides hope for the reader that it is possible to regain your inner strength and move forward."

> —**Molly Dean, LCSW, PMH-C**, owner of A New Path Psychotherapy Services

The **DBT Workbook** for

Narcissistic
Abuse *and*
Gaslighting

Dialectical Behavior Therapy Skills to Stay Emotionally Centered, Overcome Self-Doubt, and Reclaim Your Self-Worth

KATELYN BAXTER-MUSSER, LCSW, C-DBT

New Harbinger Publications, Inc.

Publisher's Note

This publication is designed to provide accurate and authoritative information in regard to the subject matter covered. It is sold with the understanding that the publisher is not engaged in rendering psychological, financial, legal, or other professional services. If expert assistance or counseling is needed, the services of a competent professional should be sought.

FSC
www.fsc.org
MIX
Paper from
responsible sources
FSC® C008955

Printed in the United States of America

26   25   24

10   9   8   7   6   5   4   3   2   1   First Printing

Contents

Foreword   v

Introduction   Welcome and a User's Guide to This Book   1

Chapter 1   Recognizing the Impact of Narcissistic Abuse and Gaslighting   5

Chapter 2   Reviewing the Application of Dialectical Behavior Therapy (DBT)   29

Chapter 3   Rediscovering Your Self-Compassion   41

Chapter 4   Rebuilding from the Foundation Up with Mindfulness Skills   57

Chapter 5   Reestablishing Trust by Coming to Your Wise Mind   71

Chapter 6   Reclaiming Your Relationship Rights with Interpersonal Effectiveness Skills   87

Chapter 7   Reconnecting to Your Emotions   103

Chapter 8   Regaining Control over Distressing Situations   121

Chapter 9   Reevaluating Your Thoughts   135

Chapter 10   Restoring Who You Are and Moving Forward   143

References   161

Foreword

Since you've picked up this book, you probably know that narcissistic abuse and gaslighting are devastating experiences in relationships. You may have dated someone who swept you off your feet like in a real-life fairy tale, only to wind up in a horror story of manipulation, lies, cheating, even theft. Maybe you were raised in a family in which a parent constantly criticized you behind closed doors, decimating your self-esteem, then telling you the problem is that you're "too sensitive." Or perhaps your boss flies into rages and undermines all your work. When you file a complaint with human resources, you're told how valuable he is to the company and "that's just how he is." Maybe a friend leaves you out of social events, and then makes sure you find out about them. When you bring this up, she says she has no idea what you're talking about. Perhaps you feel ashamed, isolated, hopeless, and self-doubting, to name just a few common outcomes of these interactions.

Unfortunately, no one is immune to the impact of narcissistic abuse and gaslighting, whether in an intimate partnership, at work, with a friend, or with their own family members. These terms, "narcissistic abuse" and "gaslighting," have become part of casual conversation and are frequently discussed in the media. Sometimes this information helps people realize that something very wrong happened or is happening in their life. Still, people struggle to get help and heal. In my practice as a clinical psychologist working with survivors of narcissistic abuse and gaslighting, I have seen over and over that individuals don't know where to turn for psychologically sound, evidenced-based help to understand their pain and learn how to rebuild their self-worth. Therefore, I'm honored to write the foreword for *The DBT Workbook for Narcissistic Abuse and Gaslighting: Dialectical Behavior Therapy Skills to Stay Emotionally Centered, Overcome Self-Doubt, and Reclaim Your Self-Worth*, by Katelyn Baxter-Musser, a book that expertly provides a path forward for survivors.

Katelyn Baxter-Musser is a nationally known expert in trauma, domestic violence, grief, relationship issues, and dialectical behavior therapy (DBT). In this book, she combines her vast skill set in a first-of-its-kind workbook to help survivors of narcissistic abuse and gaslighting understand their pain with proven strategies from psychological science.

In clear, compassionate language, Baxter-Musser describes what narcissistic abuse and gaslighting are, and what it *feels like* to get caught in their web, whether with an intimate partner, a coworker or boss, a friend, or a family member. She explains these complicated behaviors so that you, the reader, feel understood and know you are not alone. You are not the only one who has experienced the narcissist's manipulation, constant criticism, and blame, which has caused you to doubt your reality, and ultimately, your sense of who you are. When you read her stories of people who have been in your shoes, you will breathe a sigh of relief. You will know you are in good hands and are on your way to healing.

Baxter-Musser wisely chose DBT to guide her readers toward growth. One of the most robust and evidenced-based therapies in mental health, DBT is used around the world to teach people a plethora of skills to build what Marsha Linehan, the creator of DBT, calls "a life worth living." These skills include staying present in the here and now; identifying and managing emotions, including overwhelming ones; and setting healthy boundaries and communicating effectively for healthy relationships. The truth is that these are skills that all of us need to know, and you will learn skills not only for moving forward from narcissistic abuse and gaslighting, but for all parts of life.

In addition, Baxter-Musser brings in mental health strategies from beyond DBT to enhance your coping toolbox. You will learn about the value of self-compassion and how to implement it. Self-compassion is another widely established psychological tool that teaches you to turn down that internal critical voice, and in contrast, talk to yourself, in times of stress, with the kind, supportive words you would offer a friend. This practice is essential for survivors of narcissistic abuse and gaslighting: you likely have internalized the narcissist's voice, and hear it over and over in your head, in spite of your best efforts to stop it. In my own practice, it's rewarding to see the power of self-compassion as clients begin to offer the same empathy to themselves that they easily give to others.

I am so happy you are reading this wise, empathetic book, and you will be, too. In these pages, you will find Baxter-Musser's deep understanding of narcissistic abuse and gaslighting and their impact on your mental health and well-being. Baxter-Musser has taught around the country on these topics. Now you have her expertise in your hands, distilled into one volume. As the survivor, you maybe be filled with self-doubt and question your self-worth; that is the natural result of these relationships. However, it's true that knowledge is power, and this book empowers you to stop doubting yourself and your experience and to create the confidence you deserve. Good luck on your journey.

—Stephanie M. Kriesberg, PsyD

INTRODUCTION

Welcome and a User's Guide to This Book

Welcome to *The DBT Workbook for Narcissistic Abuse and Gaslighting: Dialectical Behavior Therapy Skills to Stay Emotionally Centered, Overcome Self-Doubt, and Reclaim Your Self-Worth.* Within the pages of this workbook, you'll find information and activities to help you recover and heal from the effects of narcissistic abuse and gaslighting.

I'm sure you don't need me to tell you that experiencing narcissistic abuse and tactics such as gaslighting, no matter the relationship's context, are traumatic. Recognizing that truth may be validating and, at the same time, challenging to accept. Acknowledging that you are experiencing or have experienced something traumatic and need the skills that dialectical behavior therapy (DBT) can offer can be difficult. As you acknowledge your need to heal from these experiences, it's equally important to recognize that you deserve to progress in your life with resilience and self-compassion.

We may think that abuse in relationships is strictly physical, such as hitting and punching, or verbal, such as name-calling or being threatened. And we may believe that abuse only occurs in intimate relationships. However, abuse can happen in any relationship and encompass various tactics, from manipulation to ignoring and violating boundaries, gaslighting, criticizing, guilt-tripping, and even smearing one's reputation. These forms of abuse don't leave physical marks, which can leave you questioning whether you're even experiencing abuse. Once you recognize that these are valid forms of abuse, it can be incredibly difficult to prove that you're experiencing them, and getting others to believe you and see the signs can feel like an uphill battle. To the world outside, the perpetrator is often charming, easy to get along with, and charismatic, yet they are the opposite behind closed doors, where they are cold, mean, and cruel, to say the least.

Narcissistic abuse and its tactics, such as gaslighting, lead to emotional dysregulation and the development of various trauma symptoms. This workbook will help you deal with both in several ways. As we move together through this workbook, we will explore real-life experiences of narcissistic abuse, highlighting how this form of emotional abuse can happen with intimate partners, family members, friends, and even coworkers. Reading about the real-life experiences of others can be validating and normalizing, and also challenging. Hopefully, these stories can help you recognize and remember that you are not alone in your experiences with narcissistic abuse.

Narcissistic abuse and gaslighting take a mental, emotional, and physical toll that can leave you feeling helpless, hopeless, and unworthy. This workbook is here to teach you practical and easy-to-understand DBT-based skills to manage the symptoms and aftermath of narcissistic abuse. They'll help you:

- Manage the triggers and trauma symptoms left in the wake of narcissistic abuse by bringing you back to the present moment

- Decrease self-judgments you may have formed about yourself because of the insults and criticism you experienced

- Increase self-acceptance and compassion so you can recognize that you deserve to recover and heal from an abusive relationship, and that you deserve good things in life

- Build meaningful relationships by rediscovering your needs and setting boundaries based on your values, which were discarded and minimized during your relationship

- Identify, understand, and learn to regulate difficult emotions caused by narcissistic abuse and build positive emotional experiences

- Develop healthy and adaptive coping skills

At this point, you may be thinking, *That sounds too good to be true.* Experiencing narcissistic abuse is confusing and dysregulating; often, the experience leaves people mistrusting themselves, others, and the world around them. They feel as if they may never return to who they know themselves to be. However, the effects of narcissistic abuse and tactics such as gaslighting are not permanent. Even though it may not feel like it right now, you can reestablish your sense of safety, learn to trust your instincts again, and increase your sense of self-worth. The term *neuroplasticity* refers to the brain's ability to change. Through new, positive experiences, you can rewire your brain and heal from trauma (Lovering 2022). The DBT-based skills presented in this workbook are here to help you begin this process of rewiring your brain and healing.

How to Use This Workbook

How you use this workbook is up to you. You can move through it from start to finish, or you can go to a chapter that provides the skills you need right now. (If you're feeling triggered and highly distressed, and you're struggling to cope with this moment, I recommend starting with chapter 8, "Regaining Control over Distressing Situations.") This workbook is written in such a way that you can work through it individually or with your mental health professional.

In many sections, you'll be invited to write about your experiences regarding abuse. To get the most out of this workbook, you need to feel safe responding openly to the prompts, so it's important to be mindful of where you keep the workbook and who may have access to it. To safeguard yourself, you can write in a shorthand that only you understand, keep the book with your mental health professional, or even answer the prompts in a password-protected note on your phone.

This book includes many helpful worksheets and exercises that are available for download at https://www.newharbinger.com/52892. At this website, you'll also find other free tools not included in the book. See the back of the book for more details on accessing these free tools.

Moving Forward Is Possible

Narcissistic abuse and gaslighting take so much away from you, the survivor. I am sure that you want to heal quickly, begin to move forward, and reclaim your life. At the same time, you may feel nervous about moving forward and what your life will look like. We can't rush the process of healing and recovery. As you work through this book, it's important to remember that learning, using, and applying DBT skills takes time and commitment. Be patient with yourself, and if you need extra support, seek out a qualified mental health practitioner in your area to assist you.

EXERCISE: Keeping Hope

When you've reached the end of the workbook, my hope is that you will have reclaimed yourself, your confidence, and your sense of self-worth. Even when it feels hard to keep going and implementing DBT-based skills, you can still have hope.

Using the following prompt, write one thing you hope to have reclaimed by the end of this workbook; and when moving forward gets tough, visit this page to remind yourself of what you're working toward.

By the end of this workbook, I will have reclaimed [for example, my sense of self or my ability to trust myself]

_____

_____

_____

_____

_____

This workbook is here to provide you with acknowledgment, validation, hope, and practical skills for your journey moving forward. You deserve to reclaim everything that narcissistic abuse has taken from you and find a new sense of self—as a person who has had your experiences but is not defined by them. I know it's hard to start, but you already purchased the workbook, and now you just need to take a deep breath and turn the page.

CHAPTER 1

Recognizing the Impact of Narcissistic Abuse and Gaslighting

The impact of narcissistic abuse and gaslighting runs very deep for survivors, but I'm sure you don't need me to tell you that. Your experiences have led you to this workbook, and you know that narcissistic abuse can affect all levels of your being—emotional, physical, mental, and spiritual—and that its effects often last long after the relationship has ended.

The terms *narcissistic abuse* and *gaslighting* are frequently used in the media and on social media, but what exactly are they? How do you recognize the signs of narcissistic abuse? How do you know when you're experiencing gaslighting? What defines a narcissistically abusive relationship? And most importantly, to address what brought you to this workbook, how do you recover from the effects of narcissistic abuse and gaslighting?

This workbook is here to answer these questions. But more than that, it will provide the steps you can take to recover from the impacts of narcissistic abuse and gaslighting using dialectical behavior therapy (DBT) skills. When you exit an abusive relationship, it can be challenging to know where to start with rebuilding yourself. This workbook will help you find that place and then support you on your journey of recovery and healing.

What Is Narcissistic Abuse?

Narcissistic abuse is an insidious form of emotional abuse in which the perpetrator uses abusive and manipulative behaviors to dehumanize, isolate, and control or manipulate a person's mental, behavioral, and emotional state, tearing apart their sense of self for their (the perpetrator's) personal gain. If you've ever wondered whether you're the victim of narcissistic abuse or not, you're not alone. Narcissistic abuse is challenging to identify.

Narcissistic abuse can occur in any type of relationship, be it one with a colleague, a friend, a family member, or an intimate partner. While the characteristics of narcissistic abuse in these different types of relationships may be similar, there are behaviors specific to each type of relationship that can help you determine if you're experiencing narcissistic abuse. Here's a brief summary of these different behaviors; it is not exhaustive:

- **Workplace colleagues**—a colleague or boss who puts you and your work down; bullies you; is highly critical of you; undermines your performance and professional competence; takes credit for your achievements; manipulates your career opportunities for their own gain; engages in office politics to isolate and control you; humiliates or belittles you in front of others; demeans you; disregards your time, effort, and boundaries; and targets your professional identity, causing you to doubt your skills, qualifications, and self-confidence related to your work.

- **Friendships**—a friend who prioritizes their own needs and desires, creating a one-sided relationship in which your needs are dismissed or minimized; undermines or attempts to outshine your positive experiences and successes; makes you feel that it is a privilege to be their friend; puts you down; seeks out your praise; tries to sabotage your other relationships; talks negatively about you behind your back; spreads lies and rumors to manipulate others' perceptions of you; lacks empathy; helps and supports you only when it benefits them; creates conflict and turmoil in friendships to keep the focus on them and their needs; has a constant need for validation and admiration.

- **Family members**—a family member who prioritizes their own needs; exploits and manipulates you for their gain; has unreasonable expectations; blames you for their problems; takes credit for or sabotages your successes and achievements; needs excessive attention; offers conditional love; minimizes your emotional needs; undermines your independence; pits family members against each other to divert attention away from their own behaviors; uses selective generosity to manipulate and control; violates your boundaries; disregards your need for privacy and individual autonomy; uses emotional blackmail, guilt-tripping, or threats of abandonment as tactics of manipulation and control.

- **Intimate partner**—a partner who pulls you into the relationship with love-bombing—idealizing you through excessive praise, compliments, attention, and positive gestures early in the relationship—only to later replace these behaviors with excessive devaluation and criticism; systematically isolates you from your support system, increasing your dependence on them; uses intimacy as a means to control, reward, and punish you; exhibits extreme and irrational jealously; exploits your vulnerabilities; undermines your self-confidence; withholds affection; is highly critical and demanding; uses put-downs, insults, stonewalling, and blame-shifting; and ignores your boundaries.

As you can see, there are similarities in how narcissistic abuse unfolds in different relationships, but at the end of the day, no matter the context of the relationship, three things are ultimately true about narcissistic abuse:

1. Perpetrators manipulate, use, and control others for their own benefit and gain.

2. While there are common patterns and emotional consequences shared by survivors of narcissistic abuse, it is essential to remember that your journey of healing and recovery will be unique to you.

3. You are not to blame, and this was not your fault. No matter the form, *abuse* is a choice.

Identifying as a survivor of narcissistic abuse, and sharing your experiences, can be difficult. It is okay if you feel uncertain about opening up to others about your experiences, or if you feel as though you don't know where to begin. You are in control of when and with whom you share your experiences of narcissistic abuse. It can be helpful and powerful to start sharing your experiences, even if it's just on paper. Putting words on paper validates your experiences and can allow you to begin to organize your thoughts.

EXERCISE: Strength in Stories—Surviving and Thriving After Narcissistic Abuse

To begin sharing your experiences of narcissistic abuse, respond to the following prompts.

In what relationships have you experienced this form of abuse?

_____

_____

_____

How has your life changed or improved since the abusive relationship ended?

_____

_____

_____

If the relationship hasn't ended, how might your life change if it does end?

_____

_____

_____

Dating and Narcissistic Abuse: Trisha's Story

Trisha was thirty years old and enjoyed spending time with friends and family, loved hiking, and was highly successful at her job. The only thing she felt like she was missing was a partner to share her life with. Then she met John, a thirty-four-year-old successful business owner. He was everything she'd ever dreamt of in a partner. He was tall, handsome, and intelligent, and he easily connected with all her friends; her family adored him. He texted her often, visited her frequently at work, sent her flowers, and showered her with compliments. Trisha felt like she was in a whirlwind romance straight out of a movie.

She thought it was sweet that John constantly checked in on her and wanted her to share her location on her phone to ensure that she was safe. He wanted to be with her constantly and frequently mentioned that they must be soulmates. He told her that no one else understood him like she did, and that they were meant to be together. But as time went on, the nonstop admiration faded and was replaced with belittling and constant criticism. When they had a disagreement, Trisha always found herself taking the blame. She began to feel as though she was walking on eggshells, and she would do anything to avoid upsetting John. As the days turned to months, Trisha found herself overwhelmed and worrying constantly. She realized she hadn't spoken to or seen her friends in months because John became jealous when she'd give them her attention or spend time with them.

John's manipulative tactics, subtle forms of gaslighting that he used to convince her that her friends were a threat to their relationship, left her feeling isolated. She couldn't make a decision without second-guessing herself. John's constant criticism and belittlement had eroded her self-confidence, leaving her perpetually uncertain about her choices, constantly questioning her judgments and instincts, dependent on him for the validation of her choices and decisions. She felt confused, embarrassed, sad, and alone. The narcissistic abuse had caused her to lose sight of her true self as she struggled to reconcile the person she used to be with the person that John insisted she was.

Detecting Toxic Relationships: Identifying the Signs of Narcissistic Abuse

Trisha's story is all too common. A whirlwind romance that feels too good to be true likely is too good to be true. Survivors of narcissistic abuse in intimate relationships often report that the script was flipped once they settled into the relationship and felt invested and attached. The shift from intense and undivided attention, caring, kindness, and excessive complimenting (known as love-bombing) to manipulation, insults, and gaslighting creates confusion, self-doubt, embarrassment, and other overwhelming negative emotions. It feels like having the rug pulled out from underneath you. Survivors like you are left believing that the relationship changed because there is something wrong with you: you are too sensitive, you are misinterpreting jokes, and you are not enough. This distorted narrative, a common outcome of experiencing narcissistic abuse and gaslighting, leaves you doubting your perception of reality and viewing yourself as fundamentally flawed.

You may find yourself racking your brain, trying to figure out what you did wrong or how you can get the relationship back to its initial state. Your desire to return the relationship to its original state may cause you to take responsibility for things you didn't do in an effort to avoid conflict. When you confront the perpetrator about concerns and problems, their denial of events or insistence that you're misremembering conversations triggers self-doubt, undermining your perceptions of reality. Your belief that this person loves, admires, and cares for you slowly fades, replaced with the sense that you need to walk on eggshells around them.

If the abuse occurs at work, the perpetrator may try anything to sabotage your work and professional accomplishments. The supportive workplace environment that you knew becomes toxic, filled with exploitation and undermining tactics. Your colleague may spread rumors about you, exclude you from work events, and give you backhanded compliments in front of others. They may suddenly become critical or take credit for your ideas, using subtle gaslighting techniques to cause you to question your processional competence. They are persistent and cunning in their efforts to undermine and one-up you.

In friendships and family relationships, you may find that you don't feel genuinely loved or accepted for who you are. Your value in the relationship is conditional. You are only seen or appreciated when you're an extension of the perpetrator. Your independence and individuality are dismissed, and any attempt to assert your autonomy is countered with judgment, criticism, and belittlement of who you are and what you achieve. As with perpetrators of narcissistic abuse in other relationships, they employ tactics of manipulation, projection, denial, blame-shifting, and minimization to isolate you and systematically undermine your sense of self and self-confidence.

Narcissistic abuse often begins subtly; manipulative behaviors and tactics may be hard to spot. Though your intuition may tell you that something is off or wrong in the relationship, perpetrators of narcissistic abuse are skilled at planting seeds of doubt that cause you to dismiss or brush off your concerns. As the relationship progresses, you may find yourself altering aspects of who you are to please the perpetrator and minimize conflict.

Eventually, you'll face blame, attacks on your memory, isolation, emotional minimization, and even accusations of having a personality disorder or mental health diagnosis. Many red flags may signal that something is extremely off in the relationship, but the perpetrator skillfully avoids taking responsibility and instead, through manipulation, convinces you that something's wrong with you. The insidious tactics of narcissistic abuse and gaslighting systematically isolate you from friends, family, and coworkers, leaving you feeling alone and fostering an increasing dependence on the perpetrator.

As time passes, isolation increases and the abuse intensifies, making it even more challenging for you to discern the toxic and abusive dynamics at play. The use of gaslighting increases, distorting your perception of events and leaving you to second-guess your own experiences. The perpetrator's sole focus is their needs, and your boundaries are consistently disregarded, your needs routinely pushed aside. This toxic relationship leads to an ever-increasing sense of self-doubt, causing confusion and a profound loss of trust in your own abilities. The idea of leaving the relationship or workplace is daunting because your self-esteem has been—and continues to be—eroded, and you believe you're unworthy of positive experiences and feel completely demoralized.

Narcissistic abuse can manifest in several ways, all of which can profoundly impact your mental, emotional, and physical health. Defining or putting words to an abusive experience you've had can be validating and helpful in your healing and recovery journey.

EXERCISE: Identifying Tactics of Narcissistic Abuse

Here are common tactics and characteristics of narcissistic abuse in various relationships. As you read through the list, put a checkmark next to those you've experienced.

- ☐ Verbal abuse and criticism, such as belittling, shaming, name-calling, accusing, ordering, threatening, or bullying

- ☐ Jealousy and competition: this presents as the perpetrator always having to one-up or compete with you

- ☐ Withholding: denying things such as affection, money, and sex

- ☐ Running a smear campaign: spreading lies and rumors about you

- ☐ Lying: persistent and purposeful deception

- ☐ Not accepting responsibility: twisting and turning conversations and events around in order to blame you

- ☐ Love-bombing: exaggerated attention and affection in order to influence you

☐ Sabotaging: intentional interference with your relationships with others and/or your endeavors

☐ Manipulation and controlling behaviors: this takes many forms, including deflection, diverting the conversation, and emotional blackmail, among other tactics

☐ Negative comparisons: comparing you to others or themselves in order to put you down

☐ Isolating: finding ways to pull you away from your support systems

☐ Physical violence: examples include but are not limited to hitting, destruction of your property, or preventing you from leaving

☐ Invading your privacy: going through your phone, emails, and/or material things

☐ Disrespecting boundaries: not giving you the space you've requested, not adhering to the limits you've set, not honoring the requests you've made

☐ Exploitation: taking advantage of you for their benefit with utter disregard for you

☐ Blame-shifting: making you feel responsible for their actions, problems, and mistakes

☐ Gaslighting: the perpetrator does or says things to make you distrust your perception of reality

☐ Mirroring: a manipulation tactic in which the perpetrator reflects or imitates your behaviors, characteristics, values, interests, and vulnerabilities to present as though you share the same traits, likes, dislikes, and so forth to create a false sense of compatibility

☐ Hoovering: a tactic of manipulation that "sucks" you back into the relationship

☐ Triangulation: using third parties to trigger jealousy, insecurity, and feelings of inadequacy

☐ Projection: accusing you of negative behaviors, traits, or qualities that they possess

☐ Lack of empathy: being insensitive to your needs, feelings, and general sense of well-being

☐ Favoritism: showing preferential treatment to individuals who boost their ego (such as other coworkers or family members)

☐ Inconsistent praise and criticism: shifting from praise in one moment to harsh criticism the next

☐ Unreasonable demands: making unreasonable demands of your time, resources, or attention; expecting you to prioritize them above all else

This is not an exhaustive list. Use the spaces below to identify other ways you've experienced narcissistic abuse.

☐ _____

☐ _____

☐ _____

As you reflect on the lists above, you may realize that you didn't experience just one tactic. You likely recognize that you've experienced several tactics of narcissistic abuse. You are not alone. Recall Trisha's experience. Perpetrators of narcissistic abuse will use multiple tactics—if not all tactics at their disposal—to meet their needs at the expense of your emotional, physical, and mental well-being.

Empowering Awareness: Recognizing the Stages of Narcissistic Abuse

Being engaged in a narcissistically abusive relationship feels like spinning around and around in a circle until you are so dizzy, your balance is off. But even when you stop—that is, leave the relationship—the room keeps spinning. Trying to make sense of this toxic relationship that has taken so much from you is complex and confusing. Much like Trisha did, you may grapple with a sense of disbelief about the relationship, and how you lost yourself, and not understand why it was so difficult to disengage from the relationship sooner. Knowing and understanding the stages of narcissistic abuse can help you understand why it's so challenging to exit these types of abusive relationships.

Here's a brief description of each stage of narcissistic abuse.

Stage 1: Idealization. In this stage, the perpetrator offers excessive attention, praise, compliments, affection, and admiration. The perpetrator puts you on a pedestal. You are made to feel special and cherished, as if you are the most important person in the world; and though this feels good at first, it can quickly start to feel like too much. Perpetrators often present with a high level of interest in your likes, needs, goals, and aspirations. By mirroring these aspects of who you are, the perpetrator provides a false sense of compatibility, making you feel understood and deeply connected. Mirroring ultimately reinforces that idealized image of the perpetrator whom you believe you have a deep connection with, sharing the same values, needs, and aspirations.

Stage 2: Devaluation. In the devaluation stage, there is a noticeable shift from feeling valued and cherished in the relationship to being minimized, criticized, and demeaned. The perpetrator gradually transforms from someone who was caring, kind, and thoughtful to someone who is cruel, mean, and manipulative. You begin to feel confused and insecure; you start to doubt yourself, your sanity, and your perception of reality. Through their actions and words, the perpetrator communicates that you are not good enough and are failing to meet their needs. Tactics of blame-shifting, belittling, and criticizing erode your self-esteem and self-confidence. The perpetrator shifts from idealizing and connecting with you to being cold and shut off. You may find yourself striving to revert the relationship to what it once was, not realizing that the perpetrator was being disingenuous and manipulative from the start.

Stage 3: Discard. This stage is what it sounds like: the perpetrator withdraws their attention and affection, often out of the blue, or decides they're done with you altogether. They will end the relationship abruptly and often callously. They will invalidate your experiences and emotions, blame you for the relationship ending, and attack your character. The abrupt ending of the relationship is highly emotionally distressing and can exacerbate trauma symptoms you've been experiencing.

Stage 4: Hoovering. After the relationship has ended, the perpetrator may attempt to suck you back into the abusive and toxic relationship, hence the term *hoovering*. The goal of this stage is to reengage you in the relationship. This stage is characterized by efforts to reconnect by reaching out, minimizing the problems in the relationship, manipulating you with attention and charm, reminding you of the good times and downplaying the bad.

How the relationship began and what it becomes could not be more opposite, from admiration and excitement to fear, confusion, and abuse. By the time you notice that something is wrong in the relationship, the perpetrator has drawn you in, isolated you from your support systems, chipped away at your sense of self-worth, and made you believe you are the problem and the one who is broken and flawed. You feel confused and mistrust yourself and the world around you. Not all narcissistically abusive relationships will follow the same patterns; the dynamics and tactics of abuse that perpetrators use can vary. But it is easy to be drawn in to these relationships and extremely challenging to separate from them.

Understanding the stages of narcissistic abuse is crucial to making sense of your experiences. This framework can help you comprehend the abusive relationship you endured. This knowledge not only validates and normalizes your experiences but also fosters the development of self-compassion, an essential element in healing and recovery from narcissistic abuse and gaslighting. (We will explore self-compassion in depth later.) Moreover, an understanding of the stages can help reduce the self-blame you may be experiencing.

EXERCISE: Deciphering Narcissistic Abuse—Assessing Your Experience and Emotional Response

Here's a list of common experiences that survivors of narcissistic abuse have both during and after an abusive relationship. While not an exhaustive list, it's meant to help you identify how narcissistic abuse has affected you. Mark any experiences you've had or are having.

- ☐ Feeling like you walk on eggshells

- ☐ Feeling confused

- ☐ Feeling like you are always to blame

- ☐ Feeling isolated

- ☐ Struggling to make decisions

- ☐ Feeling like you don't recognize yourself anymore

- ☐ Doubting your perceptions and reality

- ☐ Feeling powerless

☐ Feeling hopeless about your current situation and the future

☐ Having low self-esteem and self-worth

☐ Experiencing chronic stress and a heightened sense of anxiety

☐ Not trusting others

☐ Not trusting yourself

☐ Feeling not good enough

☐ Having a pervasive sense of shame

☐ Experiencing stress-related health problems

☐ Living in fear that the perpetrator will retaliate if you speak out against them

☐ Believing that it's not okay to have and set boundaries

The intensity and duration of your experiences will vary based on your specific circumstances. Regardless, an abusive relationship—or relationships—with a family member, romantic partner, or colleague brought you to this workbook. Now that you've identified specific tactics of narcissistic abuse and assessed your emotional responses, take a moment to reflect on how narcissistic abuse has impacted you.

EXERCISE: Processing the Impact of Narcissistic Abuse

Using the prompts below, write three ways that narcissistic abuse has impacted you. For example, you may struggle with self-doubt or feel like you can't trust others. It's likely there are more than three ways that narcissistic abuse has affected you, but for now focus on three, and we'll revisit them at the end of the chapter.

Narcissistic abuse has

_____

_____

Narcissistic abuse has

_____

_____

Narcissistic abuse has

_____

_____

You are not alone in dealing with the aftermath of narcissistic abuse, and future chapters will help you identify DBT-based skills you can use to heal and recover from this abuse.

Unveiling the Manipulative Tactic of Gaslighting

Of all the various tactics of narcissistic abuse, gaslighting is perhaps the most malicious, manipulative, and well-known. For these reasons, it's essential for us to dive a little deeper into this tactic and its debilitating effects.

Gaslighting is a form of psychological manipulation that causes you to question yourself, the world around you, and your sanity. Perpetrators of narcissistic abuse use it to gain power and control by causing you to doubt yourself. As you lose the ability to trust yourself, your reliance on the perpetrator increases, even to the point that you rely on them to recall memories or make decisions. Your self-trust isn't broken after just one incident of gaslighting. It's a tactic of abuse used over and over to slowly confuse you and increase your self-doubt.

Gaslighting causes you to doubt your:

- Thoughts

- Feelings

- Perceptions

- Judgments

- Memories

- Reality

Gaslighting unfolds gradually and subtly, making it challenging to identify. On top of that, perpetrators of narcissistic abuse often use several gaslighting techniques to manipulate you for their benefit. Understanding these techniques can help you recognize instances of gaslighting within past or present relationships.

- *Rewriting history and distorting reality:* Perpetrators will recreate stories in ways that make them look favorable, causing you to doubt your recollection of what happened.

- *Discrediting:* Perpetrators will spread lies and rumors about you, or they may tell you lies about what other people supposedly believe about you.

- *Lying:* Perpetrators will lie frequently. Even if you counteract a lie with proof that they are wrong, they will not back down or change their story. They will even tell you different things at different times.

- *Diverting your attention:* Perpetrators will change the subject or turn a question back on you, taking a conversation off course.

- *Denial:* Perpetrators won't take responsibility for their behaviors or actions.

- *Withholding information:* Perpetrators will withhold information to control the narrative.

- *Minimizing:* Perpetrators will minimize or discount your thoughts and feelings and tell you that how you think, feel, or act is wrong or an overreaction.

- *Smoothing out a situation with kindness:* Perpetrators will inauthentically tell you what you want to hear or use kind words to avoid taking responsibility for their actions.

- *Blame-shifting:* Perpetrators will blame you for their behaviors. Even if you know you're not at fault, this tactic will cause you to question yourself.

- *Countering:* Perpetrators will question your memory of a situation.

- *Projection:* Perpetrators will attribute their own negative qualities to you.

This is not an exhaustive list. Use the spaces below to identify other gaslighting techniques you've experienced.

- _____

- _____

The Language of Gaslighting

Perpetrators of narcissistic abuse use manipulative statements to undermine you and create confusion and self-doubt. In using such language, perpetrators seek to avoid accountability, protect their self-image, and isolate you. Being able to pinpoint gaslighting statements is critical to identifying narcissistic abuse in your current or past relationships. Moreover, you may be uncertain whether or not you experienced gaslighting in the past, and this skill can help validate that these experiences were real.

EXERCISE: Spotting Gaslighting Language

Here's a short list of gaslighting phrases that may have been used against you. Check off those you recognize. This is not an exhaustive list, so additional space is provided for you to write down statements unique to your experiences.

- ☐ You are so dramatic.

- ☐ You are overreacting.

- ☐ You are imagining things.

- ☐ It is not a big deal.

- ☐ You know you sound crazy, right?

- ☐ That never happened.

- ☐ _____

- ☐ _____

The Fun House Mirrors

Have you ever experienced fun house mirrors at a carnival? If not, imagine yourself in a room surrounded by several mirrors and looking at your various reflections. One mirror makes you look tall and skinny. Another makes you look short and round. Another makes you look like a distorted zigzag. Logically, you know what you looked like before you walked into the fun house. But now you see a mirror reflecting a different image, telling you that what you believed to be true about yourself is wrong. Which do you believe? Do you believe yourself or the evidence in front of you? The longer you stand in front of these mirrors, the easier it may be to believe that you look completely different than you thought you did.

Being in a relationship with someone who gaslights is like being in a room of funhouse mirrors. You knew yourself before you entered the relationship, but the longer you stay in it receiving distorted information about yourself, the more you question who you really are. Like those mirrors, the perpetrator creates a sense of self-doubt, and they become the person you rely on to tell you who you are, what you're thinking, and how to act. They create a world in which you begin to believe that your reality is not real, and that the perpetrator is the only one you can rely on to help you distinguish what is real and true.

Gaslighting is incredibly challenging to recognize as it is occurring. Initially, the perpetrator will lie about little things, even seemingly harmless things, such as minor details about events or conversations. But over time the amount of misinformation they communicate and the frequency with which they do it increases, poking holes in your sense of self, limiting your ability to make decisions, and creating a world that begins to feel out of your control. They may even accuse you of lying and turn your support systems against you while increasing your dependence on them. You begin to feel like everyone around you thinks you are crazy, unstable, and dishonest.

As you experience incidents of gaslighting, you may begin to have thoughts like *Am I crazy? Maybe I am the problem. There must be something wrong with me. I don't trust myself.* You may feel confused, anxious, powerless, and afraid. The feelings of self-doubt linger long after the abusive relationship has ended, sometimes causing you to question all aspects of your life. Despite the lingering self-doubt you may be experiencing right now, it is possible to trust yourself again.

Healing from gaslighting takes time, but it is both possible and worth it. You can begin this process by identifying two of your "fun house mirrors" and by reflecting on the impact that gaslighting has had on your self-perception and worldview in the following exercise.

EXERCISE: Identifying My Fun House Mirrors

Fun House Mirror 1

Write a brief description of an experience you had with gaslighting.

_____

_____

_____

_____

_____

_____

How did that experience make you feel about yourself?

_____

_____

_____

_____

_____

_____

What did that experience make you believe about yourself and your reality?

_____

_____

_____

_____

_____

When you smash the fun house mirror, what do you now recognize as the truth of that relationship?

_____

_____

_____

_____

_____

_____

Can you write a positive or empowering statement to counteract how this experience has made you feel about yourself and your reality?

_____

_____

_____

_____

Fun House Mirror 2

Write a brief description of an experience you had with gaslighting.

_____

_____

_____

_____

_____

_____

_____

How did that experience make you feel about yourself?

_____

_____

_____

_____

_____

_____

_____

What did that experience make you believe about yourself and your reality?

_____

_____

_____

_____

_____

When you smash the fun house mirror, what do you now recognize as the truth of that relationship?

_____

_____

_____

_____

_____

_____

_____

Can you write a positive or empowering statement to counteract how this experience has made you feel about yourself and your reality?

_____

_____

_____

_____

Exploring the Toll of Narcissistic Abuse and Manipulative Tactics

Narcissistic abuse is traumatizing, aligning with the Substance Abuse and Mental Health Services Administration's (2022) definition of *trauma* as an event, a series of events, or circumstances experienced by an individual that are emotionally and physically harmful and have the potential to be life threatening. Narcissistic abuse impacts your whole sense of self, affecting how you feel mentally, emotionally, and physically, with the effects often persisting long after the relationship has ended. Currently you might feel like a shell of your former self, with high levels of self-doubt and a low sense of self-worth. Your sense of safety and security in relationships and the world around you has been broken down, triggering a sense of hopelessness and helplessness.

Traumatic events bring forth biological changes, stress responses, and emotional reactions. It is important to note that not all people respond to trauma in the same ways. You may have experienced some of the trauma reactions discussed below, or maybe not. Either way, that is okay. Remember that your experiences are real, and your trauma responses make sense, given what you've experienced.

When your nervous system perceives an event as potentially dangerous, life threatening, or traumatic, a survival response—*fight, flight, freeze,* or *fawn*—is triggered as the body's natural way of surviving. One cannot override the body's survival response. It is not a conscious decision but an unconscious mechanism meant to protect you or keep you alive. Being constantly exposed to the tactics of narcissistic abuse and the techniques of gaslighting triggers the survival response in the body.

Knowing and understanding how each of these survival responses unfolds can help survivors of narcissistic abuse, such as yourself, better understand how you coped with and survived the most insidious forms of abuse:

- *Fight*—facing any perceived threat aggressively

- *Flight*—running away from the threat

- *Freeze*—being unable to move or act when faced with a threat

- *Fawn*—acting in ways to please others to avoid conflict

Being in a relationship with a perpetrator of narcissistic abuse is profoundly stressful and unpredictable. In response to this trauma, your body activates one of the above survival mechanisms instinctively; this response is beyond your conscious control. Whichever survival mechanism is activated serves to protect you from genuine threats and preserve your well-being amid the toxic and abusive dynamics you experience in a narcissistically abusive relationship.

The Lingering Impacts of Narcissistic Abuse: Physical, Mental, and Emotional Effects

There is no right way to feel after experiencing narcissistic abuse and gaslighting. Your experience is unique to you and your situation. The following table lists some of the common physical, mental, and emotional impacts of narcissistic abuse and gaslighting. Feel free to circle or highlight the ones you've experienced.

Physical Impacts	Mental Health/Emotional Impacts
Heart palpitations	Anxiety
Body aches	Depression

Physical Impacts	Mental Health/Emotional Impacts
Headaches	Post-traumatic stress disorder (PTSD)
Chronic fatigue	Complex PTSD (CPTSD)
Digestive problems	Flashbacks
Sleep problems	Low self-esteem and self-worth
Chronic stress	Difficulty trusting others
Loss of appetite	Cognitive distortions
	Shame and embarrassment
	High levels of self-doubt
	Obsessive thoughts
	Fears/Fear of abandonment
	Hopelessness
	Thoughts/Urges to self-harm and suicide
	Guilt
	Anger
	Confusion about personal boundaries
	Difficulty concentrating

Despite the difficult truths you've just confronted regarding the impacts of narcissistic abuse and gaslighting, it is crucial to remember that you are not alone in this journey. Throughout this book, I will guide you through experiences that can support you on your healing and recovery journey. Remember to pace yourself through the chapters; healing takes time, but it is a journey worth taking.

Moving Forward on the Path Toward Healing and Recovery

In this chapter, you explored many heavy topics and themes related to narcissistic abuse. This chapter may have been eye-opening. Working through it may have left you feeling like you can finally put words to your situation. The chapter's content may have been helpful but overwhelming.

As this chapter concludes, there may be lingering questions in your head. *How do I move forward? Is healing possible? Will I always feel like this?* To help answer these questions, let's review the exercise "Processing the Impact of Narcissistic Abuse" from earlier in the chapter, in which you identified three ways that narcissistic abuse has impacted you. Below you're going to add to each of those statements by identifying a goal that relates to your healing journey from narcissistic abuse and gaslighting. These personal goals will help you begin to dismantle the effects that narcissistic abuse has had on your life.

For example:

Narcissistic abuse has *caused me to doubt myself. I question everything and every choice I make.*

My goal for healing and recovery: *I want to be able to believe in myself and feel secure when I make decisions. If uncertainty arises, I want to be able to manage those emotions rather than give in to them and pull back from making that specific choice or decision.*

Now it's your turn.

Narcissistic abuse has

_____

_____

My goal for healing and recovery:

_____

_____

Narcissistic abuse has

_____

_____

My goal for healing and recovery:

_____

_____

Narcissistic abuse has

_____

_____

My goal for healing and recovery:

_____

_____

Healing from narcissistic abuse is possible; it takes time, patience, and a lot of work. You are not alone in this journey, and you have the right to smash those fun house mirrors and redefine, rebuild, and reclaim yourself. You deserve it!

CHAPTER 2

Reviewing the Application of Dialectical Behavior Therapy (DBT)

When I sit with clients who are survivors of narcissistic abuse and gaslighting in session, and we begin to put words to their experiences and feelings, there are so many moments in which they start to see that they're not crazy—that there's nothing wrong with them, and they are not to blame for the abuse they suffered. These moments begin to poke holes in their perpetrators' narratives, which have caused my clients—people who've had experiences similar to yours—to feel like they can't trust themselves, and that they are worthless. These ah-ha moments create a sense of relief. Still, they don't immediately undo the emotional toll of narcissistic abuse and gaslighting, those feelings of worthlessness, shame, and helplessness, among others. Even though the abusive relationships are over, the emotional aftereffects remain and often feel impossible to overcome.

In chapter 1, you learned about narcissistic abuse and gaslighting and their impacts on your physical and emotional well-being. As you read that chapter, I hope you felt seen, validated, and less alone in your experiences. Chapter 2 offers basic information on what DBT is, explores how DBT skills can help you in your recovery journey, and provides you with the hope that healing is possible. These skills will empower you to rediscover and rebuild your sense of self, cultivate self-compassion, establish healthy boundaries, increase your well-being, and cope with the emotional aftermath of narcissistic abuse and gaslighting.

Surfing the Emotional Waves

Imagine yourself standing in the ocean, and waves keep coming at you, knocking you over. You try to stand up, but another wave comes and knocks you down again. Standing up and finding your balance is tricky when waves keep knocking you over. You may get angry at the ocean and wish the waves would stop coming. You may get mad at yourself because you feel like you should be able to stand. "Those waves shouldn't be able to knock me down," you find yourself saying. The reality is the waves are not going to stop coming. Some days, they might not be as rough or strong, but there will always be waves; it is the ocean after all!

Sometimes, it may seem like the emotions, memories, and intrusive thoughts related to the abuse you experienced take over and fully control you. Other times, you feel in control and not flooded by the aftermath of narcissistic abuse and gaslighting. Instead, you feel settled or peaceful; the ocean is calm and there are no waves. No matter how much you like the gentleness of that experience, you know there will be times ahead in your healing and recovery journey when the waves will get choppy again. So what can you do?

> You can't stop the waves, but you can learn how to surf. —Jon Kabat-Zinn (1994, 32)

Resisting, ignoring, or allowing these waves to carry you away is not the answer to managing them; you need to learn how to surf them. The toll that narcissistic abuse and gaslighting take on you can make it feel like you'll never be able to surf these waves, like you'll never be able to recover from these negative experiences. DBT skills can help you rebuild, reclaim, and rediscover your surfboard and balance, so that when the triggers of abuse, negative thoughts, or intense emotions, such as shame, start to carry you away, you have the skills to surf through those moments. But we can't just grab a surfboard and—poof!—own the waves, right? No, learning to surf takes time. It takes focused energy, commitment, and patience.

What Is Dialectical Behavior Therapy (DBT)?

To build your DBT skills surfboard, you must first understand what DBT is, why it was developed, and how it will help you as a survivor of narcissistic abuse and gaslighting.

Pulling skills and information from various therapeutic modalities and mindfulness practices, Marsha Linehan (2015) developed DBT in the late 1970s to help people struggling with intense and difficult-to-manage emotions. DBT comprises four modules: mindfulness, interpersonal effectiveness, emotion regulation, and distress tolerance. One of the reasons DBT is so effective is that each of the four modules contains a clear set of techniques, or "skills," that are easy to understand, that are practical, and that you can begin to use immediately.

Whether you are currently in a narcissistically abusive relationship, recently left one, or even left one some time ago, you probably recognize that narcissistic abuse changes how you view yourself and the people and the world around you. The impact of narcissistic abuse can lead to various dysregulating emotional responses that feel like they impact all areas of your life.

Enter DBT! Through practice and the continued use of DBT skills, it is possible to effectively manage maladaptive responses to the overwhelming and intense emotions related to narcissistic abuse and gaslighting.

These skills encourage you to:

- Be present and increase awareness of thoughts and emotions

- Set healthy boundaries

- Develop new ways to effectively manage difficult emotions while also increasing positive emotional experiences

- Effectively manage triggers

You may feel apprehensive about learning new skills. However, you picked up this workbook looking for change, looking for a way to move forward from the psychological abuse you have endured. I know how hard it can be to be hopeful when you feel dysregulated. You may be thinking, *Well, learning new skills sounds great, but I feel too alone and broken to be helped.* One of the things that makes DBT so powerful is that it was developed by someone who really understands what it's like to struggle with intense and dysregulating emotions.

In 2011, Marsha Linehan publicly disclosed that she suffered from borderline personality disorder. At seventeen, she was self-harming and had overwhelming urges to die. She went to an inpatient mental health facility but continued to struggle with her mental health after being released. In 1967, she had an epiphany that eventually led to her attending graduate school, and it was during that time that she began the foundational work of developing DBT (Carey 2011).

It is important to note that a common misconception of DBT is that it's only for people who meet the criteria for borderline personality disorder as detailed in the *Diagnostic and Statistical Manual of Mental Disorders*, 5th edition. Nothing could be further from the truth! DBT effectively helps people who struggle with all sorts of mental health disorders, such as personality disorders, substance use disorders, anxiety, depression, post-traumatic stress disorder, and trauma. As we dive deeper into DBT-based skills in this workbook, remember that these skills were created for you by someone who has also struggled and felt helpless—even hopeless—at times. This workbook focuses on teaching you practical and effective skills for managing the effects of narcissistic abuse and gaslighting, but it also helps you to understand how to apply these skills to your healing and recovery journey. Although we'll be discussing these skills within the context of narcissistic abuse and gaslighting, they apply to many other situations in which intense and overwhelming emotions are triggered. Using these skills in a variety of situations will strengthen your agility with them!

Narcissistic Abuse, Gaslighting, and Maladaptive Coping

Being in a relationship in which you experience narcissistic abuse and gaslighting is exhausting and confusing. As you begin to feel as though you're losing touch with reality, experience thoughts of not being good enough, and feel like a shell of your former self, intense emotions such as shame, confusion, guilt, and sadness (just to name a few) will feel all-consuming. These moments of intense emotion are often accompanied by an intense urge to shut off, avoid, or numb out from the emotional pain, even if only momentarily, rather than cope effectively. Or you may find yourself responding impulsively or using maladaptive skills that help you feel better in the short term but lead to more distress in the long term. These maladaptive skills, though familiar, temporarily comforting, and fast acting, can lead to more anxiety, guilt, and shame.

In the following list of maladaptive coping skills, circle those you've found yourself engaging in due to narcissistic abuse and gaslighting. This is not an exhaustive list. In the empty spaces, write in maladaptive skills not listed that you've used to cope.

List of Maladaptive Coping Skills

- Isolating

- Not taking care of yourself (physically, mentally, emotionally)

- Not taking care of your living space

- Overeating/Not eating enough

- Oversleeping

- Using drugs or alcohol to cope

- Spending money unnecessarily

- Shutting down

- Ruminating

- _____

- _____

- _____

These unhealthy coping skills are like potholes on your healing and recovery journey. They are getting in the way of you being able to rebuild your self-confidence, ability to trust, self-acceptance, and self-compassion. But they work in the moment, right? And the idea of developing skills that will support you in managing the aftermath of the abuse may seem unachievable and daunting. Luckily, DBT has four modules to help you develop healthy skills and apply them to your life immediately.

The Four Modules of DBT

DBT comprises four modules:

- Mindfulness

- Interpersonal effectiveness

- Emotion regulation

- Distress tolerance

We'll briefly review each module, identifying how it can benefit you as a survivor of narcissistic abuse and gaslighting. Then, in subsequent chapters, we'll dive deeper into the modules and explore many DBT-based skills to support your healing.

Mindfulness

In DBT, mindfulness skills compose the foundation. The mindfulness skills you'll learn will support all the skills of the other modules. *Mindfulness* means being fully aware of the present moment. When you're mindful, you're not ruminating about the past or worrying about the future. You're aware of what is happening around and inside you. Mindfulness helps you to be more effective, to not become overwhelmed or overreact to triggers or distressing situations. Believe it or not, everyone is capable of being mindful. Mindfulness is important because it helps us to become aware of, accept, and choose how to respond to distressing or triggering moments.

MINDFULNESS, NARCISSISTIC ABUSE, AND GASLIGHTING

Narcissistic abuse and gaslighting can cause your nervous system to become stuck in survival mode. Even after the abusive relationship has ended, you continue to feel dysregulated and experience trauma symptoms. You may actively try to avoid thinking about or feeling anything related to the narcissistically abusive relationship. Trying to push away and avoid thoughts, feelings, and emotions related to the abusive relationship is counterproductive to healing.

Mindfulness can help you confront the trauma you've experienced in a way that decreases judgment and self-blame and emphasizes self-compassion. Mindfulness can support you in managing negative emotions, accepting the present moment, and reducing suffering. As you practice mindfulness, begin to recognize triggers, and become unstuck from negative thoughts or feelings such as guilt, shame, and mistrust, you can move from *reacting* to the present moment to *responding* to the present moment with awareness.

EXERCISE: Mindfulness and You

Now that you know a bit more about what mindfulness is and why it's important for healing from narcissistic abuse and gaslighting, write down one goal you have for yourself as you learn these skills and apply them to your healing process:

Example: *I want to be less reactive to my triggers.*

Goal:

_____

_____

_____

Interpersonal Effectiveness

Interpersonal effectiveness skills will help you learn what your boundaries are and then establish—or reestablish—them. These skills will help you manage conflict with others in a way that maintains your self-respect, recognize and end unhealthy relationships, and build your confidence to engage in healthy relationships.

INTERPERSONAL EFFECTIVENESS, NARCISSISTIC ABUSE, AND GASLIGHTING

Narcissistic abuse and gaslighting shift how we see ourselves in relationships and how we view others. After experiencing narcissistic abuse and gaslighting, you may find it hard to trust other people. You constantly worry about upsetting others and fear that you'll do something wrong. You may want to disengage with everyone around you, have lost sight of your boundaries, and feel that you don't have a right to set limits with others.

Mistrust, lack of self-confidence, and feeling as if your boundaries don't matter are just part of the aftermath of narcissistic abuse and gaslighting. Interpersonal effectiveness skills can help you reestablish your sense of self in relationships and rebuild and engage in healthy relationships.

EXERCISE: Interpersonal Effectiveness and You

Now that you know a bit more about interpersonal effectiveness and how its skills are important for healing from narcissistic abuse and gaslighting, write down one goal you have for yourself as you learn these skills and apply them to your healing process:

Example: *I want to be able to set healthier boundaries.*

Goal:

_____

_____

_____

Emotion Regulation

We all have emotions! Sometimes, it may feel as though your emotions control you rather than you control your emotions. DBT helps reduce our vulnerability to the dysregulating emotions that hijack our system. Learning what to do and how to respond to our emotions can be challenging. DBT-based emotion regulation skills will help you identify your emotions, recognize their purpose, and respond to them in a regulated way.

EMOTION REGULATION, NARCISSISTIC ABUSE, AND GASLIGHTING

Emotions are one way our internal systems communicate with us and the world around us. Perpetrators of narcissistic abuse and gaslighting create situations in which you feel emotionally disoriented, and over time you'll start to mistrust your internal experiences. They'll try to convince you that your emotions are wrong by minimizing and denying your emotional experiences.

Right now, it may appear that you can't trust your emotions, or you may have so many intense emotions that shutting them down feels easier than facing them. However, emotion regulation skills will help you recognize your emotions and rebuild your belief that they are valid, accurate, and essential.

EXERCISE: Emotion Regulation and You

Now that you know a bit more about what emotion regulation is and why it's important for healing from narcissistic abuse and gaslighting, write down one goal you have for yourself as you learn these skills and apply them to your healing process:

Example: *I want to understand my emotions and triggers better.*

Goal:

_____

_____

_____

Distress Tolerance

Distress tolerance helps us manage intense emotions, not by changing them or denying they exist but by accepting them. Distress tolerance skills are highly effective in helping you cope with a situation in the moment without engaging in maladaptive coping skills that could worsen the situation. These skills are not used in everyday situations. They are reserved for crises, when you're experiencing intense emotional pain, when you're unable to resolve a problem in the moment, or when you're unable to access other DBT skills.

DISTRESS TOLERANCE, NARCISSISTIC ABUSE, AND GASLIGHTING

Even if you're no longer in an abusive relationship, you may still have intrusive thoughts and emotions that trigger distress. Distress tolerance skills can support you in managing those distressing and painful thoughts and situations related to the abuse you experienced. These skills work effectively and quickly. They help you effectively cope with triggers of abuse, which in turn enhances your self-efficacy with managing your trauma triggers.

EXERCISE: Distress Tolerance and You

Now that you know a bit more about what distress tolerance is and why it's important for healing from narcissistic abuse and gaslighting, write down one goal you have for yourself as you learn these skills and apply them to your healing process:

Example: *I want to be able to manage maladaptive coping skills and replace them with adaptive skills.*

Goal:

_____

_____

_____

Dialectics

While not a module, dialectics is an essential aspect of DBT. *Dialectics* is the process of bringing together two things that seem to be in opposition. Trauma can lead to dysregulating thoughts and extreme thinking. It can be easy to get stuck in the dysregulating thoughts and beliefs that result from trauma. By taking a dialectical approach, you can become unstuck from dysregulating thoughts and extreme thinking. Bringing together two seemingly opposing ideas will help you examine a situation or thought from various perspectives. Taking a dialectical approach will help you to get unstuck from the all-or-nothing, black-and-white thinking traumatic situations can create, and from there you can begin to find a path forward on your healing and recovery journey.

While DBT has many dialectics, we will briefly focus on acceptance versus change. You may be thinking, *How can those two things relate to one another?* It's impossible to change something we haven't accepted. But, by accepting something, we are then able to change it. In terms of narcissistic abuse and gaslighting, this means first accepting who you are and how your trauma has impacted you. Acceptance requires acknowledging without judgment the validity of your pain and emotional distress caused by the narcissistic abuse you experienced. Acceptance is balanced with change. Change requires you to use the skills in this book as a guide and support—to develop a new set of problem-solving skills to help you rebuild, increase your sense of self-worth, reclaim your autonomy, and trust yourself. Dialectics allows for you to grow beyond the trauma you experienced without denying that you experienced it or minimizing the impact it had on your life.

Moving Forward on the Path Toward Healing and Recovery

You now have a deeper understanding of what lies ahead as you move through this workbook, and how the skills you'll develop can help support you, a survivor of narcissistic abuse and gaslighting. Working through this book, you will develop skills that will help you increase your self-compassion, cope with trauma-related thoughts and feelings, self-regulate, set healthy boundaries, and so much more. While your healing and recovery journey may not be easy, with these skills you will be equipped to navigate the aftermath of the abuse, grow, and emerge stronger than before.

CHAPTER 3

Rediscovering Your Self-Compassion

To say that recovery from narcissistic abuse and gaslighting is challenging would be an understatement.

However, you already know that. Narcissistic abuse impacts all aspects of your life and requires healing and recovery on many levels. As you work to begin to trust yourself and your emotions again, manage relationships, and cope with trauma-related triggers, the most important and sometimes overlooked area of healing is how you treat and view yourself.

After enduring a narcissistically abusive relationship in which you experienced gaslighting, manipulation, guilt trips, hoovering, and other tactics of narcissistic abuse, it's natural to ask some difficult questions: *How did I get here? Why did I stay? How did I miss the signs? What is wrong with me?* Rather than helping you to heal and recover from narcissistic abuse, these questions trigger feelings of shame, guilt, embarrassment, anger, and self-hatred. These emotions can feel overwhelming and never-ending. It may be difficult to believe now, but these emotions will not last forever. By developing self-compassion, it is possible to silence the critical, shaming voice that asks those questions, reduce negative emotions by acknowledging your feelings without judgment, and improve your overall well-being.

Practicing self-compassion enhances psychological well-being, happiness, optimism, and a sense of connectedness, and it decreases anxiety, depression, and rumination (Neff 2009). When you move forward from the effects of narcissistic abuse and gaslighting, it can feel like it would be easier to avoid the aftermath of the trauma, but that will only prolong your suffering. By cultivating self-compassion, you can learn to respond to yourself with kindness and empathy when facing trauma-related triggers.

Having a foundation in self-compassion will empower you to be patient with yourself as you integrate DBT skills into your everyday life. Being grounded in self-compassion will allow you to acknowledge that challenges in your healing and recovery journey are perfectly normal. For these reasons and others, self-compassion is essential in your healing and recovery from narcissistic abuse.

Narcissistic Abuse While Dating: Olivia's Story

Last year, at her friend Morgan's party, Olivia was introduced to James. They instantly connected, and James asked her on a date. Initially hesitant, Olivia eventually agreed, and the date went so much better than she could have anticipated. James was attentive, and the conversation flowed easily; they discovered they had similar interests and experiences. It was an instant connection unlike anything she'd felt before. Their romance, from meeting James to seeing him almost daily to becoming exclusive within just a few weeks, all happened very fast.

This relationship was everything Olivia had been looking for, and she and James seemed perfect together. Six months on, however, while at a friend's party, Olivia noticed a shift in James's treatment of her. Before arriving at the party, James had commented on how beautiful she looked. But then several times in conversations with friends at the party, he made negative comments about her appearance. Olivia was stunned, and on the drive home she mentioned how much he had hurt her feelings. James, however, laughed it off, pointing out that she didn't know how to take a joke and even implied that she was misremembering the conversations. This was a pivotal moment for her when, confused and hurt, she began to doubt herself.

Gradually, after that night, things began to change between them. James grew distant. He responded less often to her calls, would ignore her texts, and frequently seemed agitated and annoyed with her. When they did talk or spend time together, he belittled her work and appearance, laughed at her mistakes and insecurities, and mocked her feelings when she tried to talk about problems in their relationship. He accused her of being overbearing, needy, and overly sensitive. It didn't matter what she did or said. She always felt like she was doing something wrong, and her anxiety was becoming overwhelming. She was becoming increasingly more disappointed in herself; she struggled to sleep, felt persistent sadness, and began withdrawing from her friends.

Everything with James had been so amazing, and she wondered how she could be destroying what seemed like a perfect relationship. She felt embarrassed, angry, and unlovable and believed something was wrong with her. No matter how hard she tried, no matter what she did, things with James did not improve. She constantly walked on eggshells around James, not wanting to upset him. He grew increasingly impatient with her, telling her that something was wrong with her and that her depression and anxiety made it difficult for anyone to love her.

After their relationship ended, Olivia felt hollow and like a shell of her former self. She became aware of a voice inside her constantly reminding her that she was not enough, that she was broken and unlovable. Struggling with self-criticism, self-loathing, and a deep sense of depression, Olivia recognized that it was time to start counseling, not to salvage her relationship with James but to begin to love herself again.

Narcissistic Abuse, Gaslighting, and Self-Compassion

Overwhelming negative emotions, negative self-talk, and automatic negative thoughts are common experiences in the aftermath of narcissistic abuse. Trying to manage this aftermath without self-compassion can lead to more negative self-talk, more painful emotional responses, and even the use of unhealthy coping skills. Because of internalized self-criticism, a reduced sense of self-worth, and the fear of vulnerability after experiencing abuse, it can feel almost impossible to access self-compassion. The self-doubt and self-blame resulting from gaslighting can lead you to believe that you are not worthy or deserving of self-compassion, but nothing could be further from the truth.

Despite the painful emotions, negative self-talk, self-blame, and self-doubt, it is crucial to remember that self-compassion is a powerful tool for you to rely on throughout your healing journey. When you experience difficult, overwhelming, and challenging times in your healing and recovery from narcissistic abuse and gaslighting, self-compassion will encourage you to:

- Be kind to yourself.

- Not shame or blame yourself.

- Acknowledge your suffering and pain.

- Approach your emotional pain and suffering with understanding and patience.

- Recognize that everyone makes mistakes.

Recognizing and believing that you are worthy of self-compassion, and identifying how to incorporate it into your healing journey, are the most challenging barriers to overcome after leaving an abusive relationship. When your self-esteem is low because of narcissistic abuse, you feel worthless, broken, flawed, and confused, and you doubt yourself, as did Olivia; self-compassion is crucial in those moments but can feel like the hardest thing to cultivate.

What Is Self-Compassion?

Simply put, *self-compassion* is the genuine and authentic feelings of kindness and grace that a person offers themself. Self-compassion entails offering ourselves the same empathy we give to others for whom we care deeply. When we practice self-compassion, we acknowledge our pain, struggles, and emotions without denying them or telling ourselves that we should feel something different.

Self-compassion is not weakness, self-pity, or selfishness. Instead, it is approaching self-judgments with kindness, challenging the idea that you are alone, and recognizing that everyone suffers. It is about being mindful of your negative emotional responses and negative thoughts rather than getting lost in them (Neff 2023).

Cultivating self-compassion is not easy! Often, without hesitation we can extend compassion toward others experiencing challenges, but when faced with the same challenges, we respond with self-judgment and blame, ignoring self-compassion altogether. We can learn to cultivate self-compassion by turning the same kindness we show others inward.

Steps for Self-Compassion

In painful or difficult situations, we can extend self-compassion to ourselves by moving through the following steps (based on Neff 2023):

1. Recognize that *you* are suffering.

2. Notice the emotions that suffering brings up for you. Be aware of these emotions without becoming lost in them or trying to avoid them.

3. Respond to your suffering with caring, kindness, and warmth.

4. Offer yourself understanding, not judgment, for having pain and suffering.

5. Recognize that you are not alone in your suffering; all humans experience suffering.

To help you begin to frame how self-compassion applies to experiences of narcissistic abuse and gaslighting, let's look at these steps more closely:

1. Recognize that *you* are suffering: In this step, you allow yourself to acknowledge the emotional pain and distress caused by the abuse.

2. Respond to your suffering with caring, kindness, and warmth: Treat yourself with the same kindness you would extend to someone you care about. Use phrases that you'd use to offer support to a loved one or best friend who may be suffering, such as "I deserve support during emotionally difficult times." Practice self-care activities, such as:

   • Taking a walk in nature or going on a hike

   • Using a guided self-compassion meditation

   • Taking a soothing bath or shower

   • Reading inspirational quotes

   • Engaging in a creative activity, such as drawing or painting

   • Cuddling with your pet

3. Offer yourself understanding, not judgment, for having pain and suffering: Instead of blaming yourself for the abuse, offer yourself understanding by recognizing that the abuse was not your fault. Practice self-compassion with statements that validate your emotions and your experiences, such as:

   • It is okay to feel the way I do; my emotions are real and valid.

   • I survived something incredibly difficult, and my strength is commendable.

- I deserve kindness and understanding, especially from myself.

- The pain I feel is a natural response to the trauma I endured.

- I acknowledge the impact of the abuse on my well-being without judgment.

4. Recognize that you are not alone in your suffering; all humans experience suffering: Remind yourself that you are not alone in healing from narcissistic abuse. Remembering that others have also healed from narcissistic abuse can help decrease feelings of isolation and self-blame.

Now that we've looked at the steps you can take to practice turning compassion inward as self-compassion, let's explore some of the ways you can begin to make practicing self-compassion a regular part of your healing and recovery journey.

Self-Compassion: Your First Steps Toward Healing

Consciously shifting from self-doubt and self-blame to self-compassion is challenging. The various tactics of narcissistic abuse you've experienced can make it difficult to believe that you deserve self-compassion and, at times, even create barriers to beginning the practice of self-compassion.

To start, we can use self-compassion to focus on how we're currently feeling about and coping with our past experiences of narcissistic abuse and gaslighting. Self-compassion can help us manage negative self-talk, challenge self-blame, validate feelings, and reflect on progress. Identifying self-compassionate statements to repeat to yourself in times of distress and throughout the day will increase your sense of self-worth and build emotional resilience. Let's explore these.

EXERCISE: Empowering Self-Compassion with Affirmations

Place a checkmark next to two or three of the following self-compassion affirmations that you feel could be beneficial for where you're at right now in your healing journey. If none of these affirmations fit for you, write your own on the blank lines that are provided.

☐ I am doing my best.

☐ I am not to blame for the abuse I endured; I deserve love and healing.

☐ Other people struggle, and it is okay if I do too.

☐ It is okay to make mistakes.

☐ I am doing the best I can at this moment with the resources I have.

☐ I am allowed to feel how I feel.

☐ I am good enough.

☐ I deserve compassion and kindness.

☐ I am proud of who I am and where I'm going.

☐ I am healing from the effects of gaslighting, one step at a time, and that is a courageous journey.

☐ I can trust myself.

☐ I am worthy.

☐ I am resilient.

☐ I can strive to just be myself.

☐ It is okay if I fail.

☐ It is okay to have bad days.

☐ I choose self-compassion over self-blame, knowing that I am on the path to recovery.

☐ I can accept myself just as I am.

☐ I accept my flaws.

☐ I deserve compassion.

☐ I deserve empathy.

☐ _____

☐ _____

Once you've selected your self-compassion affirmations, it's important to begin to repeat them to yourself. Believing the affirmations may be difficult at first, and that's okay. With time you'll move from just saying them to yourself to believing in them and having them replace your negative self-talk.

Here are several ways to start practicing using self-compassion affirmations daily:

- Using a whiteboard marker, write your affirmations on the bathroom mirror, and each time you go into the bathroom, say them aloud while looking at yourself in the mirror.

- Write your affirmations on several sticky notes and place them in areas you frequent, such as in your kitchen, on your car's dashboard, or near your computer—wherever you spend the most time.

- Write down the affirmations three times when you wake up and again before bed. As you write them down, say them out loud or to yourself in your head.

- Make the affirmations the background of your phone.

- Download a positive affirmation app that will send you affirmations throughout the day.

Embracing Self-Compassion for Your Past

Looking back on your past and reflecting on your experiences with kindness, love, and self-compassion are no easy feats. Naturally, when looking back on past experiences, we have the tendency to engage in what's known as "hindsight bias." *Hindsight bias* refers to looking back on events with knowledge and information we have in the present moment. Looking back on your experiences with narcissistic abuse and gaslighting with the knowledge and information you have now can lead to judgments, self-blame, reduced self-confidence, and regret. Many survivors feel frustrated with themselves for not having seen signs of the abuse or for believing the lies the perpetrator told them. When this occurs, it can be helpful to shift away from judging your past experiences and decisions, which only increases distressing emotions, and instead respond with self-compassion.

Our past serves a purpose, because we can learn from it. Looking back at your past without self-compassion, you blame, criticize, and don't offer yourself kindness and grace.

With self-compassion, you can look back and recognize that you were doing the best you could in those moments. Responding to your past with self-compassion can help you regain control of the present moment and decrease emotional distress.

Use the following exercise when you notice yourself judging, blaming, shaming, or criticizing yourself for the past.

YOUR PAST, YOUR COMPASSION: A Guided Exercise

1. Just notice when you are thinking about the narcissistic abuse you experienced and fall into blaming, shaming, or criticizing. For example, maybe you're upset with yourself for not responding differently to the abuse or for not ending the relationship.

2. Take a deep breath and allow yourself to acknowledge your past without thinking about what you should have or could have done differently. Placing your hand on your heart, say to yourself (either out loud or in your head): *At that moment, I was doing my best. I survived that moment by using the knowledge and information available to me then.*

3. Now, take a deep breath and notice what's coming up for you. How did it feel to acknowledge your past with self-compassion? What are your thoughts? What are you feeling? Where do you notice these feelings in your body?

4. Now carry this feeling of self-compassion for your past throughout your day, and if you find yourself stuck in criticizing your past, come back to this feeling and this exercise.

Self-Compassion in Your Daily Life

It can be very easy to come to the end of the day and focus only on the negative or challenging aspects of your healing journey. However, acknowledging your successes in treating yourself with self-compassion is vital. To cultivate self-compassion, you need to practice self-compassion. Start small and be patient with yourself as you shift from shaming, blaming, and so forth to self-compassion. Practicing self-compassion each day will help self-compassion become a regular part of your routine.

EXERCISE: Treating Yourself with Kindness

Place a checkmark next to the activities for building self-compassion that appeal to you. Turn to this list when you require kindness, love, and self-compassion for yourself. If none appeal to you, please write your ideas at the end of the list.

- ☐ Intentionally and actively nurture a sense of appreciation and thankfulness for the small things in your life.
- ☐ Hug yourself.
- ☐ Meditate.
- ☐ Spend time focusing on your interests.
- ☐ Speak kindly to yourself.
- ☐ Practice mindfulness.
- ☐ Spend time in nature.
- ☐ Eat healthy and nourishing foods.
- ☐ Write a nurturing letter to yourself.
- ☐ Give yourself a hand or neck massage.
- ☐ Accept yourself just as you are in this moment.
- ☐ Recognize your successes, big and small.
- ☐ Practice positive affirmations.
- ☐ Listen to your needs.
- ☐ Treat yourself.
- ☐ Practice loving-kindness.
- ☐ _____
- ☐ _____

Extending Kindness to Yourself Through Loving-Kindness

Loving-kindness is a series of simple statements you say to yourself to cultivate feelings of compassion, kindness, and unconditional love first for yourself, then others, and finally the world around you. For your practice using this workbook, we'll focus on directing loving-kindness inward. Loving-kindness is powerful for survivors of narcissistic abuse and gaslighting for a variety of reasons:

- It helps us heal from emotional pain by fostering positive emotions.

- It promotes self-acceptance and self-love.

- It helps us develop a positive and compassionate mindset.

- It increases feelings of joy, peace, happiness, and connection.

To practice loving-kindness, say these phrases out loud or to yourself:

May I be happy.
May I be well.
May I be safe.
May I be peaceful and at ease.

As I've noted throughout this chapter, it can be challenging to cultivate self-compassion after experiencing abuse; as such, practicing loving-kindness without judgment and with patience is essential.

EXERCISE: Cultivating Self-Compassion— A Loving-Kindness Meditation

Follow these instructions to cultivate self-compassion and extend loving-kindness to yourself:

- Sit in a comfortable and relaxed position.

- Take five deep breaths, feeling free to close your eyes or keep them open.

- As you say each of the following statements, allow yourself to connect with your intention of extending unconditional kindness and self-compassion to yourself.

May I be happy.

May I be well.

May I be safe.

May I be peaceful and at ease.

- Repeat the statements twice before bringing this exercise to a close by taking five deep breaths, opening your eyes if they were closed, and remembering to carry this feeling of self-compassion that you cultivated with this exercise throughout your day.

Quieting Your Critical Inner Voice

We all have a critical inner voice that becomes more persistent after we've endured narcissistic abuse and gaslighting. This voice tells us we will never be good enough, don't deserve love, are broken or flawed, and will never be whole again. This voice causes us to question our perceptions and mistrust ourselves. For Olivia, her critical inner voice constantly reminded her that she was not good enough, that she was broken and unlovable. Your critical inner voice can have a major effect on your mental health and general well-being. In Olivia's case, constantly hearing her critical inner voice tell her these things caused her to start to experience symptoms of depression.

It is natural to want to avoid or ignore our critical inner voice. However, to paraphrase Carl Jung, *what we resist persists*. The following multilayered exercise aims to help you face your critical inner voice. It will help you identify what this voice is saying and guide you to counteract it with self-compassion. This exercise may trigger an emotional response, which is okay, but remember, the goal is to observe your thoughts without getting lost in them or pushing them away.

EXERCISE: Part 1—Mindfulness of Your Critical Inner Voice

Please feel free to modify this exercise so you can get the most from it. You can start by identifying just one thought and returning to the exercise later to identify other thoughts, if that feels best for you, or identify multiple thoughts all at once. Setting a timer for three to five minutes can also be helpful.

Follow these steps to hear what your critical inner voice is saying.

1. Sit comfortably with your eyes open or closed. Take three slow, deep breaths. We will explore your critical inner voice, which may have been shaped by narcissistic abuse, negatively affecting your self-perception.

2. When practicing mindfulness of your critical inner voice, it is important to avoid judging what it says and accepting as truth what it says. Visualizing these statements as passing clouds or leaves drifting on a river can be helpful.

3. Focus on how narcissistic abuse has affected you and notice what your critical inner voice says. It might say, *How could you let this happen?* Or *You are so stupid.* Or *You don't deserve love.*

4. Listen without absorbing these statements. Simply notice the thoughts as they pass through your mind like clouds drifting in the sky. Resist the urge to identify with these thoughts; instead, let them flow through your awareness.

5. After a few minutes, conclude by taking five deep breaths.

6. Write down at least three of your critical inner voice's statements in the space below. Please feel free write down more statements on a separate sheet of paper.

Example: My critical inner voice said, *You are weak and should have known better.*

My critical inner voice said,

_____

_____

My critical inner voice said,

_____

_____

My critical inner voice said,

_____

_____

Empowering Your Inner Self-Compassion

In the aftermath of narcissistically abusive relationships, one's critical inner voice can become persistent and difficult to quiet. For example, if you were raised by a narcissistically abusive caregiver, their actions and behaviors likely reinforced your critical inner voice, silencing your compassionate voice. No matter the context of the relationship, this critical inner voice can persist after the relationship has ended, as Olivia's did. It can be challenging to identify what to say to your critical inner voice. However, approaching this voice with the same compassion you offer to others will help you challenge it while practicing self-compassion.

EXERCISE: Part 2—Turning Compassion Inward

Write each critical inner voice statement you identified in part 1 of this exercise in the first column, then identify and write down corresponding compassionate statements for others in column 2 (If your best friend or loved one had this thought, how would you compassionately respond to them?) and self-compassionate statements in column 3 (take the thought from column 2 and put it in the form of an *I-statement*, turning the compassionate thought for others inward).

Critical Inner Voice Statements	Compassionate Statements	Self-Compassionate Statements
I am not good enough to be loved.	*You are worthy of unconditional and genuine love.*	*I am worthy of unconditional and genuine love.*

Critical Inner Voice Statements	Compassionate Statements	Self-Compassionate Statements

Enhancing Self-Compassion Every Day

Self-compassion is a crucial practice for your recovery from narcissistic abuse and gaslighting. It will enable you to apply the skills throughout this workbook with patience and nonjudgment. By fostering a kind and understanding relationship with yourself through a daily self-compassion practice, you'll rebuild your self-worth and counter the damaging effects of narcissistic abuse and gaslighting.

EXERCISE: Giving Yourself a Compassionate HAND

The acronym HAND provides easy-to-remember steps to help you turn the practice of compassion into self-compassion throughout the day:

H: *H*ow would you treat a loved one or friend?

A: *A*pproach yourself with a kind voice.

N: *N*urture yourself through small acts of kindness.

D: *D*o practice daily because you deserve it!

EXERCISE: Daily Self-Compassion Log

The Daily Self-Compassion Log is a valuable tool for tracking self-growth and healing. It's designed to help you identify and track your daily self-compassion practices, acknowledge your acts of self-compassion in the evening, and explore the emotions these actions elicit. An expanded version is included with this book's free tools and available for download at https://www.newharbinger.com/52892.

Date	**Morning Exercise** One way I can show myself self-compassion today is to _____.
	Evening Exercise Today, I showed myself self-compassion by _____. When I showed myself self-compassion, I felt _____.
Date	**Morning Exercise** One way I can show myself self-compassion today is to _____.
	Evening Exercise Today, I showed myself self-compassion by _____. When I showed myself self-compassion, I felt _____.

Moving Forward on the Path Toward Healing and Recovery

Initially, self-compassion requires frequent attention, focus, and effort. The goal is for it to become a natural response for you in challenging times, when you've made a mistake, or when your critical inner voice gets loud.

Now that we've reached the end of this chapter, I hope you can truly understand and believe that you are worthy of self-compassion. Incorporating self-compassion into your life will help you manage the negative emotional aftermath of narcissistic abuse and gaslighting and foster kindness toward yourself throughout your healing and recovery journey.

CHAPTER 4

Rebuilding from the Foundation Up with Mindfulness Skills

The pain, confusion, and emotional roller coaster resulting from being in a narcissistically abusive relationship can create a dreadful sensation that the past is the present. The resulting emotional drain can leave you shifting from numbness to intense emotional arousal. Have you ever wondered if there was something that could empower you to take control of your emotions? What about those feelings of self-blame and shame that narcissistic abuse can cause?

There is! Mindfulness. "Mindfulness" is a term that seems to be everywhere these days. Athletes, students from kindergarten to medical school, and business people are taught and practice mindfulness. Even though mindfulness is widely used and discussed, for the initiate it can be challenging to know what it is, where to start with it, and how to practice it. Mindfulness is an invaluable tool that you can use singularly or paired with other skills found in this workbook to help you heal from narcissistic abuse and gaslighting. While there are many benefits to mindfulness, in this workbook we'll focus on how mindfulness supports survivors of narcissistic abuse and gaslighting, such as yourself, throughout their healing and recovery journey.

Narcissistic Abuse and Parental Relationships: Chris's Story

Chris grew up in a household in which his mother consistently belittled him, invalidated his feelings, and unrelentingly manipulated him emotionally. She barraged him with criticism; nothing he ever accomplished was good enough. The abuse left Chris with an overwhelming sense of anxiety, inadequacy, and self-doubt. The impact of his upbringing carried over into his adult relationships, preventing him from opening up emotionally and trusting others or himself. He believed he was unworthy of love. His sense of hopelessness resulted in depression, isolation, and even urges to use unhealthy coping mechanisms.

In therapy, Chris learned about mindfulness and the potential benefits it could offer him in healing from the abuse. He learned to observe his thoughts without judgment, allowing them to flow by like fallen leaves in a rushing stream. In these moments, he became aware that the negative thoughts and judgments he'd believed and carried all his life were not truly his; he'd internalized them from his mother's toxicity. Practicing mindfulness helped him to identify the frequency and extent of the emotional manipulation that he experienced growing up. Mindfulness empowered him to replace self-criticism with self-compassion. Through guided meditations and mindfulness exercises, he was able to move beyond his feelings of unworthiness toward cultivating a new-found sense of self-worth.

Mindfulness and Your Healing Journey

As a survivor of narcissistic abuse and gaslighting, you are familiar with the various tactics of abuse that perpetrators use to distort your perceptions and instill pervasive self-doubt. Mindfulness helps you to counteract your self-doubt and distorted self-perceptions by increasing your self-awareness, allowing you to recognize when you're being manipulated and rebuild your sense of self. Mindfulness teaches you the skills to observe your emotions without judgment and accept them as accurate and valid. It is vital to reconnect with yourself and develop self-trust as you heal, and mindfulness will help you do these things.

As a survivor, you may find yourself stuck trying to make sense of your experiences with various abuse tactics, such as manipulation, gaslighting, belittling, and love-bombing. The attention to the present moment developed through mindfulness practices will help you disrupt this rumination cycle. This present-moment awareness will also help you recognize when your boundaries are being violated and help you reestablish them, increasing your self-confidence and allowing you to regulate intense emotional responses.

Ultimately, mindfulness is a big part of your healing and recovery journey; it promotes the development of self-awareness, supporting trauma healing, self-reconnection, enhanced coping strategies, and overall empowerment.

The Power of Mindfulness: Overcoming the Trauma of Narcissistic Abuse and Gaslighting

Mindfulness can be defined in many ways, from being fully present, giving your full attention to the task at hand, to allowing yourself to have a moment-to-moment awareness of your internal and external experiences. For you, a survivor of narcissistic abuse and gaslighting, mindfulness will be a crucial tool for healing, enabling you to recognize the impact that abuse has had on your mental health, general well-being, and how you're responding in the present moment. Practicing mindfulness, and becoming more aware of your triggers, may feel overwhelming, frightening, and even counterproductive to your urges to avoid anything that reminds you of the abuse. However, it will help you regulate your emotions, increase your self-compassion, and reduce rumination. Practicing mindfulness will allow you to be in the present moment, thus decreasing reactivity to trauma-related memories and emotions.

> [Mindfulness is] paying attention in a particular way: on purpose, in the present moment, and nonjudgmentally. —Jon Kabat-Zinn (1994, 4)

Everyone possesses the ability to be mindful. Using Jon Kabat-Zinn's definition of mindfulness, I'm going to break down the various aspects of mindfulness and identify how it can apply to you, a survivor of narcissistic abuse and gaslighting.

1. **Paying attention in a particular way** simply means being aware, noticing, observing, and paying attention to what is happening within and around you.

As a survivor of narcissistic abuse and gaslighting, this aspect of mindfulness requires you to learn to pay attention to your own internal experiences. This means looking inward, recognizing and observing your thoughts, emotions, and body sensations without judgment. Rather than pushing away unpleasant feelings, we can acknowledge them without trying to change or judge them. For example, rather than avoiding feelings of anxiety or self-doubt triggered by remembering past incidents of abuse, we allow ourselves to notice without judgment that we're having these feelings.

2. On purpose. The second component of mindfulness is to be deliberate and purposeful in choosing where to focus your attention.

In your healing and recovery journey from narcissistic abuse and gaslighting, this means choosing where you direct your attention. When distressing memories or triggers occur, with this skill you can purposefully turn your attention away from rumination and toward healthy coping skills.

3. In the present moment. When you are in the present moment, you are not ruminating on the past or worrying about your future.

This is especially critical for healing because it's easy to ruminate on past abuse experiences or worry about the future. When intrusive memories, judgments, negative self-talk, or fears arise, you can practice using this component of mindfulness by noticing your immediate surroundings, by using your five senses, and by redirecting your focus to your current experiences.

4. Nonjudgmentally. This last component of Jon Kabat-Zinn's definition of mindfulness entails being wholly in the present moment without evaluating it. This means that we don't jump to labeling something as "good" or "bad" or "right" or "wrong." We are consciously stepping away from our brain's automatic response of judging ourselves, our experiences, and the world around us.

For a survivor of narcissistic abuse and gaslighting, this means letting go of self-blame and self-criticism. For example, if you notice yourself thinking, *I should have seen the signs*, you can reframe this thought with self-compassion by thinking, *I did the best I could with the knowledge I had at the time*. This nonjudgmental stance helps break the cycle of self-blame often perpetuated by abusers.

Mindfulness Techniques for Coping with Trauma

The concept of practicing mindfulness, being more present, and becoming aware of triggers associated with past trauma may initially feel overwhelming and frightening. You may wonder, *Why would I want to be mindful of such traumatic experiences?* Yet, not being mindful of past traumatic experiences and their impact on you can lead to relationship problems, dysregulated emotions, increased stress, and emotional reactivity. The effects of narcissistic abuse and gaslighting can result in a heightened state of awareness that persists even after the relationship has ended, manifesting as frequent and unpredictable triggers, distressing emotions, and negative thoughts that cause you to react to the present moment from your past traumatic experiences instead of responding in the current moment.

Let's look at how we might cope with triggers related to narcissistic abuse and gaslighting with and without mindfulness skills.

Attempts to manage trauma-related thoughts, memories, and physical sensations without mindfulness:

1. Any reminder (such as specific locations, social media posts, specific words or phrases) of narcissistic abuse triggers an urge.

2. Person reaches for a coping mechanism that results in short-lived, immediate relief.

3. Feelings of guilt/shame arise.

4. Person feels more miserable and even experiences a sense of self-hatred.

Attempts to manage trauma-related thoughts, memories, and physical sensations with mindfulness:

1. Any reminder of narcissistic abuse triggers an urge.

2. Person practices mindfulness and uses a new way of coping.

3. Feelings of pride and increased self-confidence arise.

Practicing mindfulness is crucial for healing and recovering from narcissistic abuse and gaslighting. Through mindfulness, you can slow down and choose effective coping skills for managing trauma-related thoughts, memories, and physical sensations.

Mindfulness Practices

We explored mindfulness in general and how it applies to healing from narcissistic abuse and gaslighting. Let's now explore specific mindfulness activities that you can incorporate into your daily routine to manage intense emotions and enhance your inner strength. Mindfulness practices can be both formal and informal:

- Formal mindfulness practices are structured, scheduled, and intentional (for example, a body scan exercise).

- Informal mindfulness practices can be integrated into your everyday activities; they are flexible, less structured, and happen whenever you decide (for example, mindfully walking or simply being engaged in your surroundings without distractions).

Let's explore several *formal* mindfulness activities first.

Mindfulness of the Breath

Believe it or not, you always have a coping skill with you. Your breath! *Your breath is the most portable coping skill you have*, and mindfulness of the breath is a powerful skill. In terms of healing from narcissistic abuse and gaslighting, mindfulness of the breath can help you manage anxiety and emotional triggers because it is grounding. By focusing on the breath, you can gain a sense of control over your inner state, focus on the present, and reduce the impact of manipulation. Mindful breathing also promotes self-compassion, a crucial tool for healing.

There are many options when it comes to mindful breathing. Below are two simple exercises. Try them both and see what resonates with you. Other breathing exercises can be found on the Breathe and Be Well worksheet, included with this book's free tools and available for download at https://www.newharbinger.com/52892.

COLOR BREATHING

Color breathing is a terrific coping skill that combines mental imagery with intentional breathing to decrease stress. As you move through this technique, you may notice colors changing slightly as your emotions shift.

1. First, find a comfortable position and take deep but comfortable rhythmic breaths.

2. Choose a color to focus on; be sure to pick one that has meaning for you. For example, you may find purple and blue very calming and soothing, whereas orange and yellow may represent empowerment and energy.

3. Now imagine yourself surrounded by the color that elicits something specific to your current needs, be it a sense of peace, calm, stillness, or something else. The color should feel like it fills your body and wraps around you like a warm blanket.

4. As you breathe in the color of your choosing, notice it penetrate deep into your body, soothing any lingering stress, anxiety, or pain.

5. As you exhale, imagine all the negative emotions the color has captured being expelled from your body, leaving space for healing and positive feelings.

6. Repeat this technique until you feel more relaxed and at ease.

THE BREATHING SIGH

1. Breath in.

2. Breathe out through your mouth. The air will make a soft sighing sound as you let it out.

3. As you release the air from your body, relax your muscles and let go, like you are melting snow.

4. Repeat several times or for a set amount of time until you feel relaxed.

Mindfulness of the Body: Body Scan Practice

The body scan makes you aware of the present moment by having you focus on physical sensations throughout the body. This powerful mindfulness technique helps you reconnect with the physical sensations you experience in your body, increasing emotion regulation and awareness of trauma-related triggers. It also can be empowering, causing you to regain a sense of control over your own physical and emotional experiences.

1. To begin, find a comfortable position, sitting or lying in a quiet place. You may close your eyes or keep them open, whatever works best for you.

2. Centering yourself: When you are ready, take a few deep breaths and intentionally notice the rhythm of your breath. Become aware of the physical sensations you feel and any sounds you hear. This will allow you to become present in the current moment.

3. Beginning your scan: Start at your feet and slowly move your attention upward. Imagine being bathed in a warm, gentle light that relaxes you from your toes to the top of your head. Allow yourself to focus on each body part for 10 to 15 seconds and notice any sensations you feel, such as warmth, tension, or tingling. You may feel little to no sensations or many. There are no wrong sensations. The most important thing is to try and tune in to the present moment without judgment. You can accomplish this by acknowledging your feelings without trying to change them.

4. Tips for staying present: As you move your attention to each part of your body, try your best to stay within the present moment. If your mind starts to wander or if you notice any tension, gently bring your attention back to the body part you're scanning. If you notice tension in a spot, take a moment to breathe into that area and consciously relax it. Imagine the tension melting away with each exhale. It is important to be open to your feelings and intentionally release them before moving on to a new area.

5. Conclude mindfully: Once you've scanned your entire body, take a few moments to experience and notice your body as a whole. Feel the sensations in your body and the sense of relaxation that has developed.

6. Transition slowly: When you're ready to end the body scan, gradually become aware of your surroundings and gently open your eyes if they were closed.

Mindfulness to Decrease Self-Judgment

Self-judgment is just one piece of the dysregulating aftermath that comes from experiencing narcissistic abuse and gaslighting. Self-judgments can become a barrier to your healing process, keep you stuck, and prevent self-compassion. The self-judgments that Chris internalized from narcissistic abuse were automatic and unconscious; they were constantly running in the background of his mind, impacting how he viewed himself and the world around him.

Mindfully writing a self-compassion letter can be a powerful and moving practice that counteracts and contradicts the self-judgments that arise from abuse and trauma. A self-compassion letter helps and supports your healing by providing you a space to acknowledge your self-worth, validate your feelings, practice nurturing yourself, and reframe negative judgments. Ultimately a self-compassion letter can encourage you to move forward with increased self-confidence, acceptance, and compassion. When writing a self-compassion letter, it's essential to be gentle with yourself and avoid self-judgment.

1. Find a quiet and comfortable place to sit and write.

2. Begin by addressing the letter to yourself: "Dear [your name]."

3. In the letter, express your self-judgments and criticisms honestly. Write down the things you've been hard on yourself about, the areas where you feel inadequate, or any negative thoughts you've been holding on to.

4. After acknowledging these judgments, start to shift your tone. Write words of self-compassion and understanding. Imagine you are writing to a dear friend going through a difficult time.

5. Offer yourself words of kindness and encouragement. Challenge the self-judgment by providing evidence of your strengths, achievements, and positive qualities.

6. Conclude the letter with warmth and love. Sign it "Sincerely" or "With love."

Mindfulness Every Day

Now that we've covered some formal mindfulness practices, let's look at some informal practices, starting with "mindfulness every day." As its name implies, mindfulness every day empowers you to practice mindfulness with any task you engage in. The steps to practicing are straightforward and simple:

1. Choose a task.

2. Remind yourself that you want to stay grounded in that moment.

3. Fully engage in the activity by activating your senses.

4. Observe without judgment.

5. Practice self-compassion throughout the exercise.

As a survivor of narcissistic abuse and gaslighting, informal mindfulness activities, such as mindfulness every day, can help you stay grounded in the present moment, be mindful of triggers without getting lost in them, regulate emotional distress, practice self-compassion, and reclaim your autonomy. Mindfulness every day promotes healing and a connection to the present moment, which can help you let go of expectations that you should have reached a certain level of recovery from abuse or be anyone other than who you are right now.

This list offers ideas for how to incorporate mindfulness into your daily life. Place a check next to at least three mindfulness practices you'd be willing to implement in your daily routine. It's important to remember that when you engage in each practice you *pay attention on purpose, in the present moment, and nonjudgmentally.*

☐ Take a walk.

☐ Listen to music.

☐ Drive.

☐ Eat.

☐ Notice your breathing.

☐ Observe and notice what your senses are telling you.

☐ Shower.

☐ Brush your teeth.

☐ Wash the dishes.

☐ Walk your dog.

☐ Make a gratitude list.

☐ Blow bubbles.

☐ Watch your favorite television show (without looking at your phone!).

☐ Observe nature (for example, watch a leaf, look at the clouds).

☐ Drink your coffee or tea.

☐ Notice a worrisome thought for several minutes without immediately reacting to it.

☐ Sing.

☐ Play an instrument.

☐ Watch a rain- or snowstorm.

Mindfulness Log

By keeping a mindfulness log, you can track your use of mindfulness skills—formal or informal—and identify those that are most effective for you. The following log is available for download at this book's website, along with other free tools: https://www.newharbinger .com/52892.

Date	Mindfulness practice	What did I notice before the mindfulness practice?	What did I notice after the mindfulness practice?	Length of practice time
05/26	Body scan	I felt anxious and as if this pain will never leave me.	I felt calmer; my heart rate went back to normal.	5 minutes

Moving Forward on the Path Toward Healing and Recovery

Using mindfulness skills to heal and recover from narcissistic abuse and gaslighting can be scary. Confronting your trauma, identifying how it makes you feel, and recognizing your negative self-judgments can feel like impossible tasks. But the more you practice mindfulness, the easier it will become to face these challenges. Remember to practice within your window of tolerance, pace yourself, choose practices that resonate with you, and most importantly, offer yourself kindness and self-compassion as you practice.

In closing, I offer you these words again. Embodying them is imperative to cultivating self-compassion and promoting healing and recovery from narcissistic abuse and gaslighting with compassion, without striving.

Carry this *metta*, or mantra, forward with you through the rest of this workbook and beyond:

May I be happy.
May I be healthy.
May I be safe.
May I live with ease.

CHAPTER 5

Reestablishing Trust by Coming to Your Wise Mind

One of the most impactful consequences of narcissistic abuse and gaslighting is the slow erosion of your self-trust, which affects your confidence, judgments, perceptions, thoughts, and emotions. As your self-trust erodes, so does your sense of autonomy, self-worth, confidence, and independence. Rebuilding your self-trust is one of recovery's most challenging and necessary tasks. However, rebuilding your self-trust has a domino effect, improving your self-confidence, your awareness of and confidence in setting healthier boundaries, your ability to make effective decisions, and your self-acceptance with a decrease in self-judgment and feelings of shame and guilt. These ultimately lead you to value, love, and accept yourself more fully.

Narcissistic Abuse and Gaslighting at Work: Brad's Story

Brad recently landed his dream job. He was excited to join the team and to be working with people like Tom, who initially seemed friendly and genuinely interested in Brad's ideas. Shortly after starting his new job, Brad developed new ideas to streamline the team's workflow. He was very excited and shared this information with Tom one day over lunch. Brad's excitement turned to disbelief at their team meeting later in the week, when Brad's manager shared his ideas with the group but credited Tom for them. Frustrated and confused, Brad confronted Tom, who downplayed the incident and told Brad that he wasn't being a "team player."

Brad was upset and felt used but had no proof that the ideas had been his, so he decided it was best to let it go and move forward.

Since that experience, Brad's work environment has become increasingly toxic. Tom continually insults and mocks Brad through "jokes" that others laugh along with. When Brad expresses his discomfort, Tom dismisses him as "too sensitive." Brad has begun to question himself, wondering if maybe he is taking things too seriously. Tom constantly belittles Brad's contributions, undermining his sense of self-worth. Tom strategically inserts himself into Brad's meetings, creating unnecessary conflicts that have begun to ruin Brad's reputation. He recently started spreading damaging rumors about Brad's mental health and competence, further isolating Brad and eroding his self-confidence. Tom's calculated manipulation and abuse have left Brad emotionally drained and paralyzed by chronic self-doubt, whereas a few months ago he felt confident, outgoing, and motivated.

The Psychological Toll: States of Mind in Narcissistic Abuse and Gaslighting

Narcissistic abuse and gaslighting are subtle yet deeply harmful forms of emotional and psychological abuse. Brad's story serves as an example of how challenging it can be to identify such abuse. Manipulation, backhanded compliments, and jokes at your expense can fly just under the radar, causing you to question yourself and your reality. One of the defining features of narcissistic abuse is how its perpetrators use various techniques to slowly chip away at your sense of self, trust, and worth.

These covert abuse tactics are deployed in such a way that sometimes you don't even recognize that abuse is occurring until you've lost your confidence, sense of self-worth, ability to make choices aligned with your best interests, and complete sense of self. Rebuilding your ability to trust yourself again is paramount to healing, but doing so isn't simple. First, you must reacquaint yourself with what it means to trust yourself. What does that look like? How does it feel? Once you've identified what comprises self-trust, you can take the necessary steps to reclaim it.

States of Mind

Currently you may not feel connected to your inherent ability to trust yourself, but it's essential to understand that it's not permanently lost. DBT provides a set of skills aimed at helping you recognize and connect with your ability to trust in yourself, and we'll cover some of them in this book. This process involves defining and reconnecting with what's known as "wise mind" (Linehan 2015). Just as you can't dig for gold if you don't know what gold is, you can't find wise mind if you don't know what it is. It can be especially difficult to locate after you've been subjected to tactics of narcissistic abuse and gaslighting. Your primary goal is to identify and recognize your wise mind, along with your analytic and feeling minds. By doing so, you can ensure that when you find yourself in your wise mind you don't discount or ignore it.

Wise mind is not as elusive as it sounds. Everyone has the capacity for it, and no one is in it all the time (Linehan 2015). The best way to understand wise mind is first to explore the two states of mind that come together to establish wise mind: the analytic mind and feeling mind. As you can see from figure 1, wise mind is found where analytic mind and feeling mind overlap.

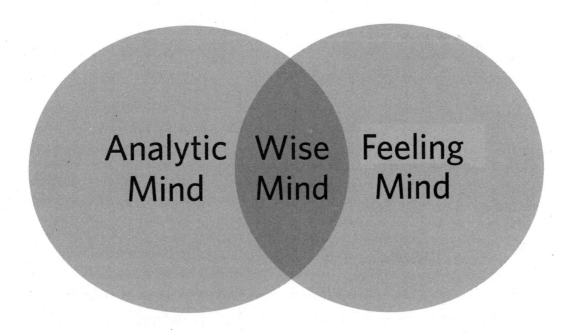

Figure 1

ANALYTIC MIND

The analytic mind is your logical, factual mind. When you're in this state of mind, you are rational. You make decisions based on facts and evidence. In this state of mind, you can make plans and evaluate situations. You are able to be calm and think logically about a situation without being overwhelmed by your emotions. Following directions is a simple example of being in analytic mind. Or, reflecting on Brad's story, he was in his analytic mind when he focused on logical ideas to streamline his team's workflow. The downside to this state of mind is that when you're in it, you ignore your emotions and thus make decisions that don't factor in emotional needs.

Analytic mind can be helpful for healing from narcissistic abuse and gaslighting. In analytic mind, you can analyze a situation factually and objectively, helping you recognize lies, manipulation, and gaslighting, which enables you to make informed decisions about your safety and well-being. Perpetrators of narcissistic abuse and gaslighting often blur, ignore, and dismiss your boundaries. Analytic mind helps you to set clear and healthy boundaries by allowing you to consider what is reasonable in relationships. In the aftermath of experiencing this abuse, you may need to make important decisions about your well-being, and accessing your analytic mind can help to facilitate an informed decision-making process.

FEELING MIND

Feeling mind is your emotional mind. When you're in this state of mind, emotions drive your actions, behaviors, and decisions without consideration of logical or rational thoughts. This state is often associated with intense emotions that can drive impulsive behaviors, and feeling mind also provides depth to your day-to-day experiences. Feeling mind, for example, is the space you'd want to be in when writing a play or a movie script. However, making decisions solely from feeling mind can lead to irrational behaviors and impulsive decisions. We saw in Brad's story that he shifted into feeling mind when he discovered that Tom took credit for his ideas, and he initially experienced emotions such as frustration, confusion, and upset.

The intense emotions produced in this state of mind can lead to heightened reactions and emotional responses that can cause you to become overwhelmed by abuse triggers. But in this state of mind, you are also able to become more aware of the full spectrum of emotions as it relates to your experiences with narcissistic abuse and gaslighting. Feeling mind helps you to process the emotional toll of experiencing this form of abuse. While experiencing narcissistic abuse and gaslighting, your emotions were discounted, denied, and ignored. Being in touch with your feeling mind encourages you to express your emotions, which can be both empowering and validating.

WISE MIND

Wise mind is a balance of your analytic mind and feeling mind paired with the intuitive knowledge of your gut, or intuition. When we're in this state of mind, we know something to be true. In this state of mind, you can bring together your feelings and logic to make healthy and effective decisions aligned with your values. Wise mind is listening to or responding to a situation from your gut instinct. It is trusting yourself. You take a balanced approach to challenges when you are in wise mind. To help you conceptualize wise mind, let's look at the following equation:

> *Awareness of your feelings + a mindful pause +*
> *knowing the facts + your gut instinct = wise mind*

The tactics of narcissistic abuse cause you to question yourself, leading you to mistrust and disbelieve your wise mind. After experiencing gaslighting, it becomes difficult to trust and believe your emotions and perceptions. These forms of abuse lead to self-doubt, which is the barrier preventing you from accessing your wise mind. For example, initially Brad was in his wise mind when he confronted Tom, demonstrating his ability to integrate both his analytic mind and feeling mind to express his frustrations. However, as his toxic work environment persisted, Brad's sense of self-worth eroded, and he became paralyzed with self-doubt. He began to struggle with balancing his analytic mind with his feeling mind, becoming stuck in his feeling mind, a justified negative emotional response to the continued manipulation and abuse he experienced at work.

Being in touch with your wise mind is important and helpful in your healing journey, and it is also important to point out that no one is in their wise mind all of the time, and that is okay. Accessing your wise mind will encourage you to validate your own reality and experiences, balance your logical analysis with emotional responses to your trauma, regulate your emotions through decreasing impulsive reactions, and promote thoughtful responses. Wise mind will help you make choices that align with your well-being, promoting a healing and recovery process that is empowering and rebuilds your sense of self.

Getting back in touch with your wise mind can be challenging at first, but by doing so you can start to rebuild your self-trust. Self-trust is believing in your own abilities, judgments, and decision-making capabilities.

When you trust yourself, you:

- Listen to your own needs

- Practice self-care and loving yourself

- Treat yourself kindly

- Allow yourself to feel your feelings without judging them

- Set healthy boundaries that you don't sacrifice to meet the needs of others

- Believe in yourself and your abilities

- Solve problems in a way that aligns with your values, morals, and goals

- Practice self-compassion

When you trust yourself, you listen to your gut, intuition, and instincts or have those aha moments. You are in wise mind. Aha moments are powerful insights that can guide you in reconnecting with and rebuilding your self-trust while helping you to understand the impact of your experiences with narcissistic abuse and gaslighting.

Some examples of aha moments as they relate to healing and recovery from narcissistic abuse and gaslighting include, but are not limited to:

- Recognizing times when you were manipulated, and understanding the tactics that were used against you

- Acknowledging that gaslighting and other tactics of abuse were not your fault, and that your emotional reactions were valid given the toxic relationship

- Connecting in your mind patterns of abusive behavior

- Understanding and believing that you are deserving and worthy of self-compassion

- Recognizing the impact of gaslighting and narcissistic abuse on your well-being

In wise mind, you may find the strength to disengage from abusive relationships. In wise mind, you recognize your worth. In wise mind, you can see the validity and truth in your thoughts and emotions.

Reconnecting with your wise mind will benefit you whether you are currently in a narcissistically abusive relationship or recently left one. When you're in wise mind, you will:

- Set healthier boundaries aligned with your values

- Establish new, healthy relationships

- Know what your needs are

- Notice an increase in your confidence

- Respond to conflicts in a balanced way versus reacting

As you reconnect with your wise mind, your self-confidence increases; you validate your experiences; you trust yourself, your decisions, and your perceptions of reality more; and you begin to rebuild your sense of autonomy.

EXERCISE: Reconnecting with Your Wise Mind— Rebuilding Self-Confidence and Healing from Abuse

Reconnecting with your wise mind—with your self-compassion and living your best life—is a powerful part of your healing and recovery journey. This exercise is designed to help you take the crucial step toward rebuilding self-confidence, emotional resilience, and inner strength by connecting to your wise mind. Identify a personal goal for yourself as you reconnect with your wise mind by finishing the prompt. The purpose of this activity is to remind yourself of what you ultimately want from your healing and recovery journey.

As I reconnect with my wise mind, my goal is to

_____

_____

_____

You can fill in the blank with a specific goal related to reconnecting with your wise mind, such as:

- As I reconnect with my wise mind, my goal is to *trust my instincts more.*

- As I reconnect with my wise mind, my goal is to *listen to my inner voice without feeling self-doubt.*

- As I reconnect with my wise mind, my goal is to *prioritize self-care and self-compassion.*

Choose a goal that empowers you and helps you keep going even when this journey is rocky.

EXERCISE: Reclaiming Your Wise Mind

Wise mind might seem elusive because maybe it's been a while since you sat with or were connected to it. So, to get you back in touch with your wise mind, let's start small. To access this state, it can be helpful to identify a previous time when you experienced wise mind. I suggest choosing a time outside of the abusive relationship. The goal is to remember a time you know you felt wise mind so you know what to look for as you begin to get in touch with your wise mind now.

A time I was in wise mind:

_____

Now explore this experience by answering these questions:

How did you know you were in wise mind?

_____

_____

What did it feel like in your body?

_____

What were your emotions?

_____

What were your thoughts?

_____

_____

_____

If you were unable to identify a time, that's okay. Be patient with yourself. Your wise mind is there. You have one; we all do. You can always come back to this activity later. Reaching wise mind is not as impossible as it may seem. The following exercise, which is included with this book's free tools and available for download at https://www.newharbinger.com/52892, can also help you access your wise mind.

EXERCISE: Wise Mind Balance Chart— Balancing Feelings and Logical Perspectives

Situation Description
Recall a specific problem that caused you emotional distress. Briefly describe the situation in which the problem occurred.

Feeling Mind

Write down the emotions you felt during this situation. Be as specific as possible, including any emotions you experienced, such as anger, sadness, anxiety, or guilt.

Analytic Mind

List the logical or rational thoughts you had during the situation. These thoughts should be based on facts, evidence, or reason.

Wise Mind Balance

Now, balance your emotional and logical sides. Consider how you could have responded to the situation in a way that took into account both your emotions and the logical aspects of the situation. What actions or decisions could have helped you find a middle ground?

The more you are in touch with your wise mind, and the more practice you have listening to it, the easier it will become to access. Remember, you will not always be in wise mind; what is important is that when you notice it, you listen to it. Reconnecting with your wise mind has a domino effect. For example, with wise mind on board, you may begin to say no to people, setting healthier boundaries, and as you do this, you start to feel good about yourself again! As your confidence increases, you begin to recognize your value and worth. That glimmer of self-worth and value can be monumental in helping you make decisions regarding the abusive relationship. That glimmer allows you to deconstruct the lies, manipulation, and deceit you've experienced and rebuild your sense of self.

Embracing Radical Acceptance

Radical acceptance is a complex and challenging skill (Linehan 2015). When we radically accept something, we're not judging it as good or bad; we simply acknowledge what is. We merely accept reality. Radical acceptance helps us move away from the self-judgment and self-blame that develop from narcissistic abuse and gaslighting. When we radically accept, we recognize the impact of the abuse, remember that we need to and want to heal, and eventually start to move forward with that journey. We practice radical acceptance while practicing self-compassion.

You might be wondering, *Why would I want to accept all the terrible things that happened to me? It's too painful.* I understand that. That said, radical acceptance is not approval. Radically accepting your experiences with narcissistic abuse and gaslighting doesn't mean being okay with what happened to you, it means saying, "It is this way. It did happen." Radical acceptance helps you acknowledge the immense pain you've experienced.

Radical acceptance takes time, patience, and nonjudgment. The trauma you've experienced from narcissistic abuse and gaslighting impacts your whole system, and as you begin to move forward, remind yourself that it's okay if you find yourself in a state of shock and disbelief. It is okay if you find that you vacillate between radical acceptance and disbelief and denial. It is normal to shift back and forth like this. This skill isn't about setting your trauma aside and saying to yourself, *Well, I just need to radically accept that.* The goal of radical acceptance is not to invalidate your feelings. Allow yourself to feel your feelings. Know that they are valid. As you move through those feelings of shock and disbelief, you'll find that you naturally shift into radical acceptance.

Quite honestly, you are already there. Just picking up this workbook was an act of radical acceptance. Even if you didn't realize it, you've already acknowledged and accepted that you experienced narcissistic abuse and gaslighting. You've already started your journey forward; you are freeing yourself from suffering and moving toward healing.

EXERCISE: Radical Acceptance Reflection

This short mindfulness-based exercise will provide you with relief in difficult situations and support you in implementing and cultivating the skill of radical acceptance.

1. Find a quiet and comfortable space to sit or lie down without distractions.

2. Take a few deep breaths. Inhale slowly through your nose for a count of 4, hold for 4, and then exhale slowly through your mouth for 4. Repeat this a few times.

3. We are going to begin by acknowledging reality. Think about a specific situation or problem that's been causing you stress or anxiety related to the abuse you've experienced. Without judgment, acknowledge that this situation is occurring. Say to yourself, *This is how things are right now, and I can radically accept it.*

4. Pay attention to the emotions that arise within you when thinking about this situation. Label these emotions without criticizing yourself for feeling them. For example, say, *I am feeling anger,* or *I am feeling sadness.*

5. Be aware of and release any resistance to the situation or urge to change it. Remind yourself that acceptance doesn't mean approval.

6. Offer yourself self-compassion. Say to yourself, *It's okay to feel this way. My emotions are valid.* Treat yourself with the same kindness and understanding you'd extend to a friend.

7. Stay present and mindful of your thoughts and feelings. Just notice them without holding on to them. If your mind starts to wander or judge, gently bring your focus back to the present moment.

8. Imagine placing the situation and your emotions in an imaginary container or balloon. Visualize letting go of this container or releasing the balloon into the sky; this symbolizes your acceptance and willingness to move forward.

9. After doing this exercise, take care of yourself by doing a self-care activity. This list of activities is not exhaustive; in the blank spaces, please feel free to write down—and then use—your favorite self-care activity.

- Listen to your favorite music.

- Engage in an activity that you are passionate about.

- Stretch gently or do yoga.

- Take a walk or spend time in nature.

- Treat yourself to a cup of tea, coffee, hot cocoa, or warm water with lemon.

- _____

- _____

Remember that radical acceptance is an ongoing process, and it's okay to return to this skill as often as needed to deal with challenging situations.

You may not always have the time to do this formal exercise in the moment, yet you may still need to use radical acceptance. Below is a list of general radical acceptance coping statements followed by statements specific to healing from narcissistic abuse and gaslighting. When you find yourself resisting reality or slipping into self-blame and judgment, you can repeat these statements to yourself or aloud to help guide you toward radical acceptance. Not all of these statements may resonate with you. Circle or highlight two that do. There is also space for you to include one or two radical acceptance coping statements in your own words.

General Radical Acceptance Coping Statements

- There is no use fighting the past.

- Right here is where I am supposed to be.

- It is what it is.

- I won't stress over the things I cannot change.

- This feeling will pass, and I will be okay.

- I cannot change what has already happened.

- It is okay to feel _____, and I can deal with it effectively by _____.

- I am only in control of my reactions now, and that is all.

- This situation is only temporary.

Radical Acceptance Coping Statements for Narcissistic Abuse and Gaslighting Recovery

- I did not deserve the abuse I experienced, but I deserve to heal and find peace.

- I am not defined by the lies and manipulation of the narcissist.

- I acknowledge the pain I've endured and am taking steps to heal.

- I am strong, resilient, and capable of reclaiming my life.

- I choose to focus on my own well-being and growth.

- I trust my own perception and intuition.

- I am breaking free from the cycle of abuse and manipulation.

- I refuse to let the past define my future.

- I am learning and growing every day, and that's a powerful journey.

- _____

- _____

Moving Forward on the Path Toward Healing and Recovery

Because of narcissistic abuse and gaslighting, you most likely shifted from feeling good, excited, and happy in your relationship to questioning yourself and your abilities, and to feeling unworthy and damaged. Over time, you may have found yourself relying on the perpetrator's account of events and situations more and more because you no longer trusted yourself. You may have isolated yourself and disengaged from others because you felt worthless. In that relationship, and even in experiences you have now outside of that relationship, you may feel as though you can't rebuild yourself, as if you are alone and that you will be a shell of your former self forever. You may feel like you'll never be able to trust your perceptions, thoughts, and emotions again. Or you may feel like you aren't good enough to experience self-love and healthy relationships.

With radical acceptance, and by reconnecting with your wise mind, you *can* move beyond this place in which you feel overwhelmed by negative emotions and unable to believe in yourself, your worth, and your abilities. If you practice these skills, your self-trust will begin to surface again, and as your belief in yourself returns, you'll have the strength to practice self-compassion, set healthy boundaries, and trust your emotional experiences. With your newfound understanding of wise mind and radical acceptance, let's move forward and develop other skills necessary for growth, healing, and recovery.

CHAPTER 6

Reclaiming Your Relationship Rights with Interpersonal Effectiveness Skills

The process of healing and recovering from narcissistic abuse has many challenges. Whether you're rebuilding your self-trust, reconnecting with your emotions, or reestablishing healthy relationships, mastering DBT-based skills requires patience, vulnerability, and the understanding that you deserve and are capable of healing and recovery.

If, at this point, the idea of reengaging in relationships feels a bit scary, do not worry; you are not alone. Many survivors of narcissistic abuse, such as yourself, report a sense of anxiety, hypervigilance, and even dread when thinking about future relationships. How could you not? You were engaged in a relationship in which your needs were dismissed; your boundaries were ignored; and your rights to feel safe, happy, and secure were slowly taken away without you even realizing it.

Being scared or hesitant about future relationships with intimate partners, family members, friends, or colleagues—or even swearing them off altogether—makes sense given everything you've been through. You may find yourself oscillating between wanting to avoid future relationships at all costs to longing for connection. Worrying about experiencing narcissistic abuse, being able to set and maintain your boundaries, advocating for your needs, and even being able to say no are some of the concerns you may have when thinking about reengaging in relationships. Feeling damaged, broken, or unworthy can make you believe you don't deserve healthy relationships. The idea of getting close to and trusting anyone again, be it a friend, coworker, or intimate partner, can feel like an insurmountable hurdle.

We all need relationships in our lives, and while avoiding relationships in the short term makes you feel safe, in the long term it can lead to depression, isolation, and general life dis-satisfaction. Healthy relationships can reduce your stress and increase your sense of happiness and general life satisfaction.

Although you may feel like you want to avoid relationships at all costs, you don't have to. You deserve to have happy, healthy relationships that foster a sense of safety and respect. In this chapter, you'll identify and build your interpersonal effectiveness skills by rediscovering your rights in relationships, recognizing your boundaries, and learning how to assert yourself in relationships by asking for what you want and saying no to what you don't want.

Narcissistic Abuse in a Friendship: Lee's Story

Lee had always considered himself a kind and caring friend. In his circle of friends, he was the go-to person when someone needed help or just a good laugh. Three months ago, he met Amanda through mutual acquaintances. They realized they shared common interests and instantly got along, bonding over their similar professions.

What began as just seeing each other when they crossed paths quickly escalated into a close friendship. To Lee it seemed that Amanda always had urgent problems to discuss, and he was the one she'd call. He did his best to help her deal with these situations, but as time went on her needs became draining. No matter how much time and effort Lee devoted to helping her, Amanda always demanded more. Their friendship shifted when Lee's mother received a breast cancer diagnosis. Lee needed support, someone to talk to, and a shoulder to lean on during this difficult time. He reached out to Amanda multiple times, only to realize that she consistently redirected their conversations back to herself. When he pointed this out, she shockingly accused him of being a selfish, inconsiderate friend who was abandoning her.

One weekend a mutual friend hosted a party, and since Lee wasn't traveling home to see his mother, he decided to attend. He tried to reach out to Amanda, but she ignored his texts. At the party, she made brief eye contact with him before purposefully looking away and continuing her conversation with someone else. At one point in the evening, he overheard her making passive-aggressive comments about him choosing his family over friends. Lee ignored the comments. After that night, whenever their group of friends was together, Amanda seemed to take every opportunity to belittle Lee, making jokes about his appearance, job, and hobbies. Lee was deeply hurt, and when he confronted Amanda, she brushed his concerns off, insisting he needed to develop a sense of humor and not take everything so seriously.

No longer able to ignore her behavior, Lee realized he was in a one-sided, toxic, and narcissistically abusive friendship. This newfound awareness left him angry and disappointed in himself for not having recognized the signs sooner. He had never considered the possibility of such toxicity in a friendship. Unfortunately, one-sided, toxic relationships can be hard to identify early in their development, and Lee would continue to develop toxic friendships with others.

Narcissistic Abuse, Gaslighting, and Healthy Relationships

Perpetrators of narcissistic abuse twist, distort, and manipulate the legitimate needs, desires, and boundaries of others to serve their own agenda. Even when you set entirely reasonable limits or clearly define your needs, they employ tactics such as minimization, denial, and gaslighting to cause you to question your sanity and convince you that *you* are the toxic and unhealthy one in the relationship. As they continue to tear you down, your sense of self-worth disappears, and you may even begin to believe that you are the problem. This narcissistic abuse can create profound confusion regarding the dynamics of healthy relationships.

Whether you're currently in or recently ended a narcissistically abusive relationship with a friend, family member, coworker, or intimate partner, the impact of the abuse you experienced can have a ripple effect on current and future relationships. You may find that in your relationships you:

- Have lost your confidence

- Are worried that you are too sensitive

- Are scared of rejection

- Have general anxiety about relationships

- Feel as though you don't know how to participate in relationships

- Have difficulty trusting others

- Feel paranoid

- Worry about missing potential signs of abuse

- Feel edgy

- Chronically overapologize

- Experience negative self-talk

- Need constant reassurance

- Have poor boundaries

- Disengage or isolate

If after reading this list you're thinking *I've experienced every one of these*, don't worry; that doesn't mean you can't develop skills that will help you have healthy relationships in the future. Healthy relationships are possible after experiencing narcissistic abuse.

Keys to Cultivating Healthy and Fulfilling Relationships

Narcissistic abuse and gaslighting can significantly distort our idea of what is and isn't healthy in relationships. As such, defining what makes up healthy relationships is critical before looking at how this abuse has impacted your current relationships and sense of future ones. Knowing what constitutes a healthy relationship will help you better evaluate the relationships you're currently nurturing and, more importantly, discern those that deserve a place in your life.

All healthy relationships—whether with friends, family members, coworkers, or intimate partners—require many overlapping foundational elements:

- Honesty

- Mutual respect

- Open communication

- Healthy boundaries

- Respect of boundaries

- Trust

- Respect of each other's individuality

- Willingness to compromise

- Equality

Before we cover the interpersonal effectiveness skills you can implement to foster healthy relationships, complete the following self-reflection exercise.

EXERCISE: Relationship Reflection #1

If it feels challenging to acknowledge that narcissistic abuse has impacted your current relationships and feelings about future ones, you are not alone. Many survivors report feeling angry or hateful toward their perpetrator for having taken away their basic sense of safety in relationships. This activity will help you identify how narcissistic abuse has impacted your current or potential future relationships.

What impact has narcissistic abuse had on your current relationships? (For example, *I feel like I can't trust people, so I avoid getting close to people*.)

_____

_____

_____

_____

How has experiencing narcissistic abuse shaped your perspective or feelings about future relationships? (For example, *There's a persistent fear that I'll encounter someone else with similar narcissistic traits, which leads me to be overly critical or suspicious of a potential partner's intentions.*)

_____

_____

_____

_____

How do you feel about yourself in relationships? (For example, *I will never be able to trust my intuition about a person again.*)

_____

_____

_____

_____

Understanding Interpersonal Effectiveness Skills

DBT-based interpersonal effectiveness skills will help you to:

- Build healthy relationships and end toxic and destructive ones

- Recognize your values and boundaries

- Remind yourself that "No" is a complete sentence (you are allowed to say no and not feel guilty afterward)

- Teach yourself how to ask for something you need because *your needs matter*

- Be effective in relationships without sacrificing your self-respect

Developing these interpersonal effectiveness skills is fundamental to your healing and recovery journey, setting the foundation for healthier interactions and personal growth.

Now, let's go over the trio of interpersonal effectiveness skills that will be able to help you do just that.

Building Your Interpersonal Effectiveness Skills

All healthy relationships—whether with friends, family members, coworkers, or intimate partners—require many overlapping foundational elements. We are going to focus on three crucial elements in relationships that are often attacked, dismissed, and distorted by perpetrators of narcissistic abuse and gaslighting: values, boundaries, and how you effectively communicate them.

Values

Your core values help you to know what you believe in and what is important to you. You can think of them like your own personal code of ethics. Core values help you to build healthy relationships and make effective decisions. When you engage in relationships or make decisions based on your core values, you feel good, you develop your sense of self-respect, and you can be proud of yourself for how you handle situations, no matter the outcome.

You may be having trouble getting in touch with your core values as a result of narcissistic abuse. This is not your fault. Perpetrators of narcissistic abuse are skilled at making you question and ignore your values so that their needs become the focus of the relationship, or they convince you that your values are invalid. Even though your core values have been bulldozed and overshadowed by the perpetrator's needs and desires, you still have them.

EXERCISE: Identifying Your Core Values

Let's identify some of your core values. Place a checkmark next to the core values that align with who you are and how you want to be in relationships. Once you've done that, circle the values you seek in others. If there are important core values missing from the list, please feel free to write them in the list or use the Expanded Core Values List offered with this book's free tools, available for download at https://www.newharbinger.com/52892.

Core Values List

☐ Integrity

☐ Honesty

☐ Respect

☐ Responsibility

☐ Accountability

☐ Empathy

☐ Adaptability

☐ Courage

☐ Family oriented

☐ Freedom

☐ Justice

☐ Spirituality

☐ Adventure

☐ Balance

☐ Independence

☐ Excellence

☐ Loyalty

☐ Patience

☐ Gratitude

☐ Kindness

☐ Fairness

☐ Tolerance

☐ Humility

☐ Generosity

☐ Creativity

☐ Open-mindedness

☐ Authenticity

☐ Leadership

☐ Perseverance

☐ Self-discipline

☐ Trustworthiness

☐ _____

☐ _____

EXERCISE: Relationship Reflection #2

Think of some healthy and positive relationships you've had in your life with friends, coaches, coworkers, family members, and so forth. Choose one relationship and reflect on it by answering the following questions.

How did that relationship make you feel?

_____

_____

_____

What were some of the positive qualities or characteristics of that relationship?

_____

_____

_____

Using that relationship as a guide, and the core values you identified above, what do you value in relationships?

_____

_____

_____

Again, using that relationship as a guide, and considering the impact that narcissistic abuse and gaslighting has had on you, how have these abusive experiences affected your values in relationships?

_____

_____

_____

In what ways do you envision yourself redefining or reinforcing your core values moving forward with current and future relationships?

_____

_____

_____

Boundaries

Boundaries are the guidelines you establish in relationships, setting limits both for yourself and for others. Rooted in your values, boundaries help you to recognize and identify your comfort level in relationships and provide clarity on your preferences and dislikes. Boundaries are critical in relationships, allowing us to participate in them in ways that are congruent with our values. They are a form of self-care, ensuring that we don't lose ourselves in a relationship, becoming overly dependent upon someone, and vice versa—that is, we don't allow somebody to become overly dependent upon us. Boundaries are based on factors personal to each of us, such as upbringing, culture, and past experiences.

Examining, rediscovering, and redefining your boundaries are key to developing your interpersonal effectiveness skills as you work to build a sense of safety, security, and stability in relationships. After experiencing narcissistic abuse, it may feel as though your boundaries are nonexistent, or that you don't have the right to set them. You may struggle to identify your boundaries or feel uncertain about setting them, fearing they'll be ignored or that you'll be punished for having them. For example, though Lee was a caring and supportive friend, Amanda consistently crossed his boundaries and manipulated their friendship for her own needs, leaving him uncertain if he had the right to have boundaries in the first place. Narcissistic abuse and gaslighting erode your sense of self-worth and make it difficult to establish boundaries and recognize when they're being violated or dismissed. These relationships are emotionally draining, and setting boundaries is essential for maintaining your well-being.

The exercise below can help increase your comfort with identifying and setting boundaries.

EXERCISE: Identifying and Setting Personal Boundaries

List your boundaries: Identify five boundaries that are important to you. For example:

- *I should be able to say no.*

- *My feelings are valid and should be acknowledged.*

- _____

- _____

- _____

- _____

- _____

Identify past experiences when your boundaries were violated or ignored in relationships in which you experienced narcissistic abuse and gaslighting: If you're comfortable doing so, and it seems possible, write down a few specific examples of past experiences when your boundaries were disregarded or violated. The purpose of this exercise is to assist you in recognizing and acknowledging times when your boundaries were disregarded.

_____

_____

_____

_____

_____

Rewrite your boundaries: Using I-statements, rewrite each boundary you listed above to clearly and assertively express your needs and expectations. For example:

- *I will say no when I need to, without feeling guilty.*

- *I will acknowledge and validate my feelings.*

- _____

- _____

- _____

- _____

- _____

Practice setting your boundaries: To increase your comfort and effectiveness with setting boundaries, practice assertive communication. Read aloud the boundary statements you created just now to help you feel more comfortable and confident asserting your boundaries. It can help to practice in front of a mirror.

After experiencing narcissistic abuse, it's common to experience uncertainty when identifying and establishing boundaries. Your body's awareness can be a helpful tool to guide you through this process. For example, have you ever had that pit-in-your-stomach feeling? The sensation of knowing something doesn't feel right, and that you are uncomfortable? This feeling can serve as a sign that you want to pay attention to your emotions and respond to the situation in a way that aligns with your values and boundaries.

Communication

After you've been in a narcissistically abusive relationship, asking for what you want and saying no may not feel like rights you have, but I assure you that you do have these rights. Your needs have most likely been denied and minimized so much that, at this point, you're not even sure how to ask for what you need. You may feel scared, lose sight of what you're asking for, and even ignore your needs.

The DEAR ME skill (based on Linehan 2015) can help you effectively communicate your wants and needs and remember that they are based on your boundaries and grounded in your values.

The acronym DEAR ME outlines steps for making a request or saying no to a request:

Define: The first step is to define the situation by just sticking to the facts.

Example: *My dad belittles my accomplishments and constantly compares me to others.*

Express: Next, express how you feel about the situation.

Example: *I feel anxious and worthless.*

Ask: Now that you've defined the situation and expressed yourself, ask for what you want.

Example: *I want you to stop comparing me to others and belittling my accomplishments.*

Reinforce: Finally, you want to reinforce your request, focusing on how meeting your request benefits all parties.

Example: *Setting this boundary is essential for my mental health; I cannot continue to be expected to share things with you, come to family events, and have a relationship with you if this continues.*

The ME part of the acronym reminds you of important things to keep in mind when making a request:

Maintain a mindful approach: You must be aware of your tone, body language, timing, and environment when asking for your request.

Everyone's boundaries matter: When making a request, remember that everyone has limits and boundaries. You can ask for your needs to be met, and others are allowed to say no. You can negotiate with others, but don't compromise your values when doing so. If a relationship is causing you to compromise your values, you may need to evaluate the healthiness of that relationship in your life.

EXERCISE: Crafting a DEAR ME Moment

Now it's your turn. Think of a boundary request you'd like to make and write it out using DEAR ME.

Define:

_____

_____

Express:

_____

_____

Ask:

_____

_____

Reinforce:

_____

_____

Maintain a mindful approach: *What things should you be aware of regarding your tone, body language, timing, and environment when making your request?*

_____

_____

Everyone's boundaries matter: *What will you do if the other person says no or tries to negotiate with you about your request?*

_____

_____

Your Relationship Bill of Rights

Identifying your rights in a relationship can be confusing after experiencing narcissistic abuse. It can be challenging to remember that you have fundamental rights in relationships. The Relationship Bill of Rights (adapted from Bourne 2020) is here to remind you of your right to have healthy and safe relationships in which you feel heard and respected:

- I have the right to ask for what I need in my relationships.

- I have the right to say no in my relationships.

- I have the right to set boundaries.

- I have the right to stick to my core values.

- I have the right to feel how I feel.

- I have the right to make decisions for myself.

- I have the right to spend time with other people.

- I have the right to my own space and autonomy.

- I have the right to be emotionally, physically, and mentally safe in relationships.

- I have the right to not be abused.

- I have the right to be treated with kindness.

- I have the right to be treated with dignity and respect.

- I have the right to be happy.

- I have the right to end a relationship that is no longer healthy or effective for my life.

Narcissistic abuse makes you question all aspects of yourself, including your rights in relationships. When you feel overwhelmed or confused about the rights you're entitled to, you can return to the Relationship Bill of Rights to help you remember what you deserve.

EXERCISE: Identifying Your Relationship Goals

Now that you have a firm understanding of how narcissistic abuse has impacted your relationships, and you can see the benefits of using interpersonal effectiveness skills, identify two goals for yourself in relationships moving forward.

Example: *I want to feel confident saying no to others.*

Goal 1:

_____

_____

Goal 2:

_____

_____

Moving Forward on the Path Toward Healing and Recovery

Interpersonal effectiveness skills are here to help you reclaim yourself in relationships and reconnect with others in ways that build your self-respect, confidence, and self-worth. As we end this chapter, hopefully you find that you've reconnected with your values and boundaries and recognize and believe that your needs matter in relationships. You deserve to feel happy and safe in all aspects of your life; your relationships are no exception.

CHAPTER 7

Reconnecting to Your Emotions

Being in a relationship in which you experience narcissistic abuse and gaslighting is like riding an emotional roller coaster, with its high highs and extremely low lows. Initially, you may experience moments when you feel loved, appreciated, and valued. However, as time unfolds, these positive feelings gradually erode and are replaced by unfounded accusations, blame-shifting, minimization of your experiences, and escalating conflict. Feelings such as anger, hatred, sadness, guilt, and shame replace your once positive emotions, leaving you with a sense of confusion and longing to feel happiness again.

Narcissistic abuse and gaslighting lead you to mistrust and question your emotions and their accuracy. You may begin to think, *Maybe I am too sensitive. Maybe there is something wrong with how I react.* You may even look outward, relying on the perpetrator to help you navigate your emotional responses and provide validation. Perpetrators often will use these moments to further exploit, demean, and manipulate you.

Even after you step off the emotional roller coaster, it can feel as if you are mentally and emotionally still on the ride. However, you can break free of this feeling by developing and implementing emotion regulation skills to help you manage distressing emotions more effectively and build positive emotional experiences.

Narcissistic Abuse in a Marriage: Blake's Story

Blake and Amelia have been married for six years, and while on the outside their relationship looks close to perfect, behind closed doors there is ongoing emotional abuse. Blake has always been sensitive, but there has never been anyone who can exploit his emotions quite like Amelia. She often belittles him, criticizing his appearance, career, and dreams. She mocks his hobbies, scoffs at his aspirations, and takes every opportunity to undermine his confidence. For example, Blake spent several hours preparing a special supper for their anniversary one evening. Amelia walked into the kitchen and disgustedly commented, "Is this the best you can do?" Blake's heart sank, and he struggled to hold back tears.

Amelia's emotional abuse has only escalated over the years. At this point, she controls every aspect of his life, from his finances to the few friends she allows him to see. She has slowly isolated him from his family and reminds him regularly of how lucky he is to have her. Blake feels trapped, powerless, and hopeless. He's unable to sleep, and his anxiety and depression are growing worse.

Recently, after a vicious argument, Blake decided he needed professional support. He has been meeting with a therapist who is teaching him that it's okay to feel his emotions, but that he also needs healthier coping methods. "You feel this way because it is this way," she says, and that powerful statement has helped him to recognize just how severe the abuse at home has become.

Understanding Narcissistic Abuse, Gaslighting, and Emotion Dysregulation

Our emotions are crucial for helping us to participate effectively in relationships, recognize our boundaries and limits, and understand the importance of our values. Our emotions tell us how we feel about ourselves, people, and the world around us. Our emotions serve a purpose; they are essential. They motivate us to act and communicate to others valuable information about our feelings (Linehan 2015). They act as our internal alarm system, providing helpful information, letting us know when we have experienced something that makes us feel good, and helping us recognize when we've experienced something hurtful or harmful. When our internal alarm system functions correctly and sends us accurate messages, we can trust our emotions and use them to guide our actions. But when it's malfunctioning, our emotions can feel overwhelming, dysregulating, and confusing.

Research has found that experiencing trauma, such as narcissistic abuse and gaslighting, impacts our ability to control and regulate negative emotions, resulting in avoidance behaviors and unhealthy coping mechanisms (Shepherd and Wild 2014; Short et al. 2018). The constant exposure to the ongoing trauma related to this abuse keeps your nervous system stuck in a survival response, which over time results in changes to areas of your brain, such as the hippocampus and amygdala, impacting how you process, store, and cope with emotionally charged memories (Bremner and Wittbrodt 2020).

The trauma resulting from narcissistic abuse leads to problems with labeling, understanding, and managing emotions, otherwise known as *emotion dysregulation*. When our emotions are dysregulated, we may experience outbursts of anger, have mood swings, or even feel stuck in our emotional state (for example, depression). Emotions that once seemed tolerable will feel insurmountable and all-consuming.

Understanding Your Emotional Responses

It is common to have a lot of complex emotions after experiencing narcissistic abuse and gaslighting. These complex emotional responses can make identifying, regulating, and coping with your emotions challenging. You may notice that you have a lot of emotions but struggle to determine what you are feeling. The first step in managing trauma-related emotions is to identify and describe the emotions you're experiencing—positive or negative. The following list can be a helpful resource for doing this. There are many ways to describe emotional experiences, but this list focuses explicitly on those typically felt by survivors of narcissistic abuse and gaslighting. Throughout this chapter, you can refer to this list when you need help identifying your emotions.

Confusion

Bewilderment

Uncertainty

Disorientation

Perplexity

Distress

Fluster

Anxiety

Nervousness

Tension

Worry

Apprehension

Agitation

Unease

Depression

Despondency

Hopelessness

Melancholy

Sadness

Despair

Sorrow

Guilt

Remorse

Self-reproach

Regret

Contrition

Shamefulness

Self-blame

Shame

Embarrassment

Humiliation

Disgrace

Inferiority

Self-consciousness

Mortification

Anger

Rage

Fury

Resentment

Hostility

Irritation

Wrath

Fear

Dread

Terror

Panic

Fright

Alarm

Horror

Uncertainty

Hesitation

Distrust

Insecurity

Indecision

Mistrust

Suspicion

Skepticism

Wariness

Cynicism

Doubt

Emotional Numbness

Apathy

Detachment

Emotionlessness

Numbness

Indifference

Blankness

Loss

Bereavement

Deprivation

Forfeiture

Deficiency

Shortage

Depletion

Grief

Sorrow

Mourning

Heartache

Desolation

Lamentation

Bereavement

Powerlessness

Helplessness

Impotence

Vulnerability

Ineffectiveness

Weakness

Incapacity

Desperation

Hopelessness

Despair

Futility

Urgency

Agony

Helplessness

Loneliness

Alienation

Relief

Comfort

Easement

Relaxation

Reprieve

Liberation

Alleviation

Hope

Optimism

Belief

Trust

Anticipation

Positivity

Confidence

Cultivating Self-Validation

The road to rebuilding and reconnecting to your emotions will not be without challenges. As such, you must practice self-validation alongside your emotion regulation skills.

> *Self-validation* means recognizing and accepting your emotions as valid and legitimate.

When we practice self-validation, we listen to and acknowledge our emotions, beliefs, and experiences without seeking validation from others. While you're building emotional resilience after experiencing narcissistic abuse and gaslighting, self-validation will support you in turning inward and trusting your instincts, reducing self-blame, and fostering self-compassion. Self-validation is crucial to your healing journey, helping you rebuild faith and trust in yourself and your emotional responses.

Allow Your Emotions with SELF-Validation

Healing and recovery from narcissistic abuse takes time. Sometimes, denying or avoiding emotions related to the abuse you suffered may feel easier. Other times, you may question yourself, wondering if your emotional responses are too intense, justifiable, or just plain wrong. Nothing is more important during these moments than remembering that there is no right way to feel and that your emotions are real and matter. Pushing away, avoiding, and questioning your feelings only leads to more emotional turmoil, but pausing and practicing SELF-validation can help you build self-confidence, regulate your emotions, and increase your awareness of trauma responses.

When you find yourself doubting, denying, or downplaying your emotional reactions related to narcissistic abuse and gaslighting, use the acronym SELF-validation to validate them:

S—Slow down and identify.

- When you feel overwhelmed by emotions related to narcissistic abuse and gaslighting, slow down, pause, and take a deep breath.

- Allow yourself a moment to identify and label the current emotion you're experiencing (for example, anxious, sad, angry).

E—Embrace without judgment.

- Accept your emotions without judging, avoiding, or suppressing them.

- Understand that your feelings are valid and a natural response to the abuse that you experienced.

L—Legitimate validation comes from within.

- Remind yourself that you don't need validation from others for your emotions to be real and to matter.

- Remember that your emotions are legitimate simply because you are experiencing them.

F—Foster favorable statements.

- Challenge the negative thoughts you're having, replacing them with compassionate and validating statements about your emotions.

- When you're questioning yourself or experiencing self-doubt, tell yourself, *It is okay to feel this way. My emotions and experiences are valid.*

EXERCISE: Acknowledge and Embrace Your Emotions with SELF-Validation

This exercise encourages you to validate the emotions you're feeling on your healing and recovery journey from narcissistic abuse and gaslighting. In this exercise, you'll foster an awareness of these emotions and self-compassion for them. First, take a look at an example of this process using Blake's story, then use the following prompts to *acknowledge* and *embrace* your own emotional responses.

Identify the situation related to narcissistic abuse or gaslighting that has triggered an emotional response: *I spent several hours preparing a special supper for our anniversary, and Amelia walked into the kitchen and said, "Is this the best that you can do?" I struggled to hold back tears.*

Now, instead of dismissing, denying, or questioning your emotion, use SELF-Validation.

S—Slow down and identify: Take a moment to reflect on the specific situation. Using the space provided, identify what emotions come to mind when you remember the hurtful comments, interactions, or criticism. Are you feeling sadness, disappointment, anger, or something else? *When I recall the anniversary supper I made, I feel sadness and disappointment.*

E—Embrace without judgment: Acknowledge the emotions you identified. How do you typically react to these emotions? Are there any patterns to your responses that you've noticed? *Typically, I try to hold back tears and minimize the impact of hurtful comments by brushing them off or ignoring them. I have noticed that I tend to internalize criticism.*

L—Legitimate validation comes from within: Remind yourself that your feelings are valid and that you don't need external validation. Identify ways you've sought validation from others in similar situations. How can you shift toward trusting your own emotions? *I often seek validation from Amelia. I am always hoping that she will see and appreciate my efforts. Moving toward trusting my own emotions means recognizing that my feelings are valid even if she doesn't acknowledge them.*

F—Foster favorable statements: Create compassionate and validating statements for yourself. Identify positive and affirming words you can use to counteract the hurtful, painful, or critical comments and interactions you experienced. *It is okay to feel sad and be disappointed. My emotions are real, are valid, and matter.*

Now you give it a try. (A printable version of this worksheet is available for download with this book's other free tools at https://www.newharbinger.com/52892.)

Identify the situation related to narcissistic abuse or gaslighting that has triggered an emotional response:

_____

_____

Now, instead of dismissing, denying, or questioning your emotion, use SELF-Validation.

S—Slow down and identify: Take a moment to reflect on the specific situation. Using the space provided, identify what emotions come to mind when you remember the hurtful comments, interactions, or criticism. Are you feeling sadness, disappointment, anger, or something else?

_____

_____

_____

E—Embrace without judgment: Acknowledge the emotions you identified. How do you typically react to these emotions? Are there any patterns to your responses that you've noticed?

_____

_____

_____

L—Legitimate validation comes from within: Remind yourself that your feelings are valid and that you don't need external validation. Identify ways you've sought validation from others in similar situations. How can you shift toward trusting your own emotions?

_____

_____

_____

F—Foster favorable statements: Create compassionate and validating statements for yourself. Identify positive and affirming words you can use to counteract the hurtful, painful, or critical comments and interactions you experienced. For example, *It is okay to feel [your emotions]. My emotions are real, and I am on a journey toward healing.*

_____

_____

_____

Developing self-validation skills requires time and patience. The manipulative techniques used in narcissistic abuse, combined with constant invalidation, can significantly undermine your self-confidence, creating a sense of self-doubt that makes it challenging to practice self-validation. You can use these affirmations to confront and overcome this self-doubt.

Self-Validation Affirmations

- My feelings are valid.

- I am allowed to feel how I feel.

- I am worthy.

- My emotions serve a purpose.

- I do not need to justify my emotions to others.

- I am giving myself permission to feel [insert emotion].

- It is okay to honor my emotions and take a self-care break.

- I am in control of how I respond to my emotions.

- I allow myself to feel my emotions without judging, ignoring, or suppressing them.

- I recognize that acknowledging my emotions is integral to my healing and recovery journey from narcissistic abuse and gaslighting.

In your own words, using the following spaces, write three of your own self-validation statements to encourage yourself to embrace and express your emotions without self-criticism.

1. _____

2. _____

3. _____

Connecting the DOTS: How Thoughts, Body Sensations, and Urges Define Emotions

Emotions are a whole system response comprising thoughts, body sensations, and urges (Linehan 2015). But after experiencing narcissistic abuse and gaslighting, trusting your thoughts, body sensations, and urges is extremely difficult. As you strive to minimize self-doubt and rebuild your confidence and trust in your emotional responses, connecting the DOTS can guide you through the steps necessary to recognize the interconnections among the various components of your emotional reactions. A downloadable worksheet for this skill is included with this book's free tools, which are available for download at https://www.new harbinger.com/52892.

Before we explore this skill, it's important to mention that you can use it in a variety of different circumstances, including those that occur after an abusive relationship has ended.

D: Describe the situation; stick to the facts and don't make assumptions or judgments.

Example: *I have been in a relationship for nine months and have noticed patterns of criticism, manipulation, and minimization and denial of my feelings. Today, during an argument, my partner criticized my appearance, intelligence, and hobbies.*

O: Observe what is happening in your body (for example, racing heart, clenched fists, and so forth).

Example: *My body felt tense, and I felt like I was about to cry. My heart was racing, my fists were clenched, and I felt a knot in my stomach.*

T: Take time to notice your thoughts. What are you thinking at this moment? Are your thoughts negative, positive, or neutral?

Example: *I experienced a lot of negative thoughts. I kept ruminating on the negative comments, wondering if they were true, and I started to doubt my self-worth.*

S: Scale the intensity level of the emotion you felt (on a scale from 0, no intensity, to 10, the highest level of this emotion you've ever experienced). Scaling your emotions can help you gauge the strength of your emotional response.

Example: *0   1   2   3   4   5   6   7   **8**   9   10*

Once you've connected the DOTS, answer the following questions.

What urges did you have in response to the situation?

Example: *I tried to stand up for myself, express my feelings, and state my boundaries so they would not treat me like this. But my urge to withdraw and protect myself emotionally was stronger. I wanted to run away because I just wanted the criticism to stop.*

What did you do? Did you act on those urges or do something else? What happened as a result of your actions?

Example: *I left the situation. I wanted to stand up for myself, but our arguments tend to go in circles, and they accuse me of lying and belittle me. So, instead, I set a boundary, stating that I needed some time alone. I reached out to my best friend, and they supported me and helped me to counteract the self-doubt I was feeling.*

Using the information gathered above, identify the emotion you're feeling now?

Example: *So much sadness.*

Using the emotions list from earlier in the chapter, are there other words to describe how you're feeling now?

I feel sad, powerless, miserable, and hurt.

EXERCISE: Connecting the DOTS

Use the steps below to help you identify and label your emotional experiences to improve emotion regulation.

D: Describe the situation; stick to the facts and don't make assumptions or judgments.

_____

_____

_____

O: Observe what is happening in your body (for example, racing heart, clenched fists, and so forth).

_____

_____

_____

T: Take time to notice your thoughts. What are you thinking at this moment? Are your thoughts negative, positive, or neutral?

_____

_____

_____

S: Scale the intensity level of the emotion you felt (on a scale from 0, no intensity, to 10, the highest level of this emotion you've ever experienced). Scaling your emotions can help you gauge the strength of your emotional response.

0   1   2   3   4   5   6   7   8   9   10

What urges did you have in response to the situation? For example, if you were angry, you may have wanted to yell.

_____

_____

_____

What did you do? Did you act on those urges or do something else? What happened as a result of your actions?

_____

_____

_____

Using the information gathered above, identify the emotion you're feeling now.

_____

Using the emotions list from chapter 7, are there other words to describe how you're feeling now?

_____

Riding the Wave to Regulate

Now that you've been introduced to the skill of connecting DOTS, which will help you identify emotions related to particular trauma experiences, it's time to develop skills to help you cope with *managing* these emotions. Experiencing narcissistic abuse and tactics such as gaslighting profoundly alters your worldview. The resulting emotion dysregulation can lead to ineffective expressions of your emotions, resulting in greater emotional pain and suffering. Trauma responses and triggers become a part of your everyday experience, causing your feelings to feel out of control. Because of this dysregulation, it may seem easier to suppress and reject your emotional experiences rather than feel them and acknowledge that you're in pain and suffering. The idea of fully embracing and allowing yourself to feel your emotions may be frightening. Trauma survivors often worry that their negative emotions will overwhelm them and fear that they'll become flooded with negative emotions if they don't minimize, ignore, or push them away.

The next time you're feeling negative emotions associated with your trauma, rather than avoiding, denying, or pushing them away, try imagining them as waves. Riding the wave is a DBT technique that encourages you to acknowledge and accept emotions without succumbing to impulsive reactions or avoidance (Linehan 2015). Rather than avoiding the waves or allowing them to knock you down, try surfing them! Here's how.

1. **Become aware of your emotion:** acknowledge and name the emotion you are feeling.

2. **Allow yourself to experience the emotion:** just observe and notice the sensations associated with your emotion.

3. **Remind yourself that you are not the emotion:** do not judge or resist the emotion; remember that just like a wave breaks on the shore, your emotion will also have an end.

4. **Ride the wave:** fully accept the emotion; close your eyes and visualize yourself riding the emotional wave, using mindfulness as needed to help ground you in the present moment.

By acknowledging your emotions and allowing them to wash over you without resistance or impulsive responses, you will become more skilled at managing and regulating them. Riding an emotional wave takes time, patience, and practice, but it can develop into a highly effective tool to help you cope with trauma reactions over time and trust in your emotional experiences, leading to healing and recovery from the effects of narcissistic abuse and gaslighting. You can and will reclaim your power over your emotions.

Managing Your Emotions by Acting Opposite

If left unaddressed, the intense and often overwhelming emotions—such as shame, anger, anxiety, fear, and so forth—you've experienced because of narcissistic abuse and gaslighting can harm your emotional health and general sense of well-being. Acting opposite, based on Linehan's (2015) opposite action skill, offers you a way to effectively respond to your emotions, empowering you to counteract the sense of helplessness you may feel when facing your emotions and deciding how to respond to them. Acting opposite:

- Validates the emotion you're experiencing in response to a trigger of your abuse

- Helps you to recognize that reacting to that emotion may not be effective

- Encourages you to identify an opposite feeling that is more adaptive

You should use this skill when your goal is to change or regulate your emotional response in situations where your emotional reaction is harmful or unhelpful, or its intensity doesn't fit the moment. For example, if you're feeling shame, the opposite emotion might be self-compassion. Acting opposite can benefit you when you're still in an abusive relationship or after one has ended:

- **In the relationship,** acting opposite can counteract manipulation and distress. For example, if the perpetrator tries to make you feel guilty, you can consciously practice asserting yourself and setting boundaries.

- **After the relationship has ended,** acting opposite can help you reframe and replace negative emotions with healthier ones. For example, if you feel shame, you can work on building self-esteem rather than criticizing yourself.

Here are the steps to acting opposite (based on Linehan 2015):

1. **Recognize the emotion:** identify an unhelpful emotion you're feeling in a specific situation.

2. **Identify the opposite emotion:** determine the opposite or more adaptive emotion to counter your initial feeling in that situation.

3. **Choose to act on the opposite emotion:** behave in a way consistent with the opposite emotion—this means doing the opposite of your initial emotional urge.

4. **Act mindfully:** stay present and be mindful of your behavior and emotions.

5. **Practice:** practice acting opposite to help change your emotional responses over time.

This chart highlights some common emotions people experience due to narcissistic abuse and gaslighting, including a way to act opposite.

Emotion	Acting Opposite
Confusion	Seek clarity through exploration and understanding.
Anger	Practice self-soothing to avoid impulsivity or aggression.
Frustration	Practice patience, adapt, or take breaks.
Guilt	Challenge and reevaluate; focus on self-compassion.
Anxiety	Engage in relaxation techniques and gradual confrontation.
Depression	Engage in pleasurable activities to challenge negative thoughts.
Isolation	Reach out to others for support and connection.
Self-doubt	Practice self-affirmation and challenge negative self-talk.
Shame	Share feelings, practice self-compassion, and challenge negative beliefs.
Sadness	Engage in mood-lifting activities and seek enjoyment.

Building Positive Experiences and Thriving After Narcissistic Abuse

Healing and recovery after narcissistic abuse can be incredibly challenging. Positive emotions can feel elusive and unobtainable. While it may seem impossible that you'll feel positive emotions again, it's crucial to remember that building positive experiences and thriving after narcissistic abuse is not only possible, it's essential for your well-being. Positive emotions help to counteract the adverse effects of narcissistic abuse and gaslighting, and eliciting those feelings by nurturing positive experiences can help you regain happiness, joy, and a sense of self-worth.

You can engage in both short- and long-term activities regularly to build positive experiences and elicit positive emotions (Linehan 2015). In the following chart, you'll find suggestions to use in your practice, and there are blank spaces for you to identify other activities you enjoy.

Short-Term Positive Experiences	Long-Term Positive Experiences
Practice gratitude.	Identify your values and live by them.
Listen to music.	Attend to relationships.
Watch a funny movie.	Create action steps to reach your goals.
Go for a walk in nature.	Create a plan to get your dream job.

BUILDING POSITIVE EXPERIENCES LOG

Utilize this log to track how you're building positive experiences and to identify the positive outcomes of engaging in these activities. This log is included with this book's free tools and available for download at https://www.newharbinger.com/52892.

Date	How did I build a positive experience?	The type of positive experience I built today!	What positive emotions did this activity make me feel?
		☐ Short-term ☐ Long-term	
		☐ Short-term ☐ Long-term	
		☐ Short-term ☐ Long-term	
		☐ Short-term ☐ Long-term	
		☐ Short-term ☐ Long-term	
		☐ Short-term ☐ Long-term	
		☐ Short-term ☐ Long-term	

Moving Forward on the Path Toward Healing and Recovery

In this chapter, you learned various skills for identifying and regulating your emotions and rebuilding your trust in your emotional experiences. Trusting your emotions is challenging and requires conscious effort and time. Over time, these emotion regulation skills will become easier to access, and you will come to a place where you know without a doubt that your emotional responses are valid. This sense of knowing marks a significant moment in your healing journey, indicating that you are reclaiming your true self and that the tactics of narcissistic abuse and gaslighting are losing their grip on you.

CHAPTER 8

Regaining Control over Distressing Situations

Narcissistic abuse and gaslighting can cause you to feel like your life is spinning out of control. Situations that once felt manageable instead lead you over a waterfall of distress. Places where you once felt joy and happiness now flood you with memories of the abuse you survived, and you find it difficult to trust the people around you. It's not just the external world that doesn't feel safe anymore; internally, you feel dysregulated and uneasy. Thoughts, emotions, physical sensations, sounds, and smells also *trigger* you. You experience a sense of uncertainty that convinces you that overwhelming and distressing emotions will last forever. To cope with these triggering experiences, you may shut down, go numb, or even turn to unhealthy coping mechanisms that only cause you more emotional pain in the long run. In these moments, it can feel as though you are barely surviving.

As a survivor of narcissistic abuse and gaslighting, triggering experiences are probably not uncommon for you. Whether you've experienced many or just one, you know how frightening they can be. Triggers of your trauma hijack you from the present moment and flood your whole system with memories of abuse. In an ideal world, you'd be able to tell yourself that you're no longer back in that moment experiencing the abuse; your brain would just stop thinking about it, and you'd just move on. Unfortunately, it's not this easy. Instead, and often without much warning, trauma triggers bring your mind back to the past, reactivating your survival mode to protect you and keep you safe, even if you're not currently in danger.

When your emotional distress is so overwhelming that it may lead to a crisis, or you are not regulated enough to implement your emotion regulation skills, turning to DBT-based distress tolerance skills can be highly effective for becoming regulated again (Linehan 2015). It's not possible to avoid every potential trauma trigger, but it is possible to develop a set of short-term skills you can use in a variety of settings to help you manage the mental, physical, and emotional impacts of triggers. These skills will also help you resist unhealthy means of coping.

Narcissistic Abuse with a Family Member: Steve's Story

As kids, Steve looked up to his older brother, Ryan. After Steve graduated from college, however, Ryan became so antagonistic toward him that the relationship felt unbearable. When they were around each other, Ryan belittled Steve, questioning his life choices, the amount of money he made, and even whom he dated. As a result, Steve mostly kept his distance from Ryan, but recently he had to see him at their parents' anniversary party. In front of their entire family and Steve's date, Ryan proceeded to attack Steve, suggesting that he wasn't intelligent enough for the recent promotion he'd received, while at the same time seemingly taking credit for Steve's accomplishment. Ryan proceeded to humiliate Steve through a series of backhanded compliments and by sharing embarrassing childhood stories.

Steve felt overwhelmed by strong emotions of anger, hurt, and embarrassment, and though he wanted to respond, he recognized that doing so while his emotions were so intense would only escalate the situation. Regretfully, he left the party early. Frustrated with how he responded to Ryan at the party, Steve recognized that he needed support. He sought out a therapist to help him develop skills to manage the high levels of distress he felt around Ryan so that going forward he could regulate his emotions and set healthy boundaries.

Understanding Triggers of Narcissistic Abuse and Gaslighting

Through their behavior, narcissistically abusive people like Steve create and maintain a state of hyperarousal and hypervigilance for survivors such as yourself and Ryan. The unpredictability of what they'll say and how they will react leaves you wondering, *What version of this person am I going to be interacting with today?* As the relationship progresses, more and more of your time is spent worrying about your interactions with them. It feels as if you're walking on eggshells. You alter what you do and how you act for fear of how they'll respond. Your nervous system becomes fine-tuned to the perpetrator's tone of voice, words, body language, and facial expressions. You feel on guard around them, constantly trying to be one step ahead of them to avoid potential conflict or deescalate conflict once it's started. The intermittent reinforcement pattern of moments of cruelty and then kindness or affection keeps your body stuck in survival mode. Over time, even after the relationship has ended, you can become stuck in this persistent state in which your nervous system responds to the world around you.

What Are Triggers?

A *trigger* is anything that reminds you of the abuse you experienced. Trigger responses range in severity depending upon the person, their traumatic experiences, and the nature of the trigger. There are internal and external triggers, and the following chart will help you to understand the difference between the two.

Internal Triggers	External Triggers
• Thoughts	• People
• Emotions	• Places
• Physical sensations	• Smells
• Feeling	• Sounds
• Beliefs/Self-criticism	• Something someone says
• Nightmares	• A specific date
	• TV/Media/Social media

The distress and dysregulation stemming from trauma triggers come on quickly and overwhelm your whole system. When traumatic experiences, such as narcissistic abuse and gaslighting, are triggered, your brain can't tell if you're back in that traumatic situation or safe in the present moment. The thinking part of your brain (prefrontal cortex) goes offline, and the limbic system, specifically your amygdala, is activated, triggering your fight, flight, freeze, or fawn response (Arnsten, Mazure, and Sinha 2012). Your brain's response is typically intense, and you'll experience distressing emotions such as panic, shame, helplessness, and fear along with physical reactions such as, but not limited to, shortness of breath, heart palpitations, upset stomach, sweating, and clenching of the jaw. In those challenging moments, you feel like you are reliving a traumatic experience. The distress tolerance skills you're going to develop in this chapter will become invaluable in helping you regain control over your emotional and physical responses while fostering a sense of control, safety, and empowerment.

From Surviving to Thriving: Using Distress Tolerance Skills with Narcissistic Abuse

Developing distress tolerance skills isn't just about adding skills to your toolbox so you can heal from narcissistic abuse and gaslighting. They can help you regain control over your life, stop the world from feeling like it's spinning out of control, and free you from the continued impact of the perpetrator. Sometimes we cope by avoiding, denying, or suppressing our emotions, which can inadvertently increase our suffering. Distress tolerance skills can increase your resilience in difficult and triggering moments, enabling you to manage overwhelming experiences so you have the strength to set boundaries, maintain self-worth, and ultimately thrive, even in the face of relentless manipulation and gaslighting.

Distress tolerance skills are critical to your healing and recovery process because they are practical, help you to cope with painful situations in the moment, and act fast. They pair well with other skills you've learned in this workbook, increasing your effectiveness in applying those skills. There are many distress tolerance skills to choose from, so if one doesn't work for you, or if after using one you're a little less distressed but still need more support, you can use a different distress tolerance skill to help you manage your emotions. Before we get into the skills themselves, you first need to identify your default coping methods.

EXERCISE: Identifying Your Usual Coping Methods

Let's identify and evaluate the current coping methods you use to manage triggers related to narcissistic abuse. This exercise will provide insight into your default response patterns when faced with distressing situations in which you may feel intense and distressing emotions such as anger, fear, and shame, to name a few. Recognizing that your typical coping mechanisms may not be effective or adaptive in these situations is the first step toward increasing your ability to tolerate distress. Using the examples from Steve as a guide, in the following chart write in your own responses.

Coping Method	Frequency	Effectiveness	Feelings and Outcomes
List the coping methods (including activities, behaviors, or thought patterns) you commonly use when faced with distress and dysregulating emotions related to narcissistic abuse and gaslighting.	Rate how often you use each coping method on a scale from 1 (rarely) to 5 (frequently).	Using a scale from 1 (not effective) to 5 (very effective), assess how effectively each coping method is for managing distress resulting from triggers related to narcissistic abuse and gaslighting.	Reflect on how each coping method makes you feel and whether there are positive or negative outcomes from using these methods.
I tend to keep my distance from Ryan, avoiding confrontations and emotional distress.	4	2	*Provides temporary relief but doesn't address the underlying issues between me and Ryan, leaving me feeling isolated and unassertive.*

Coping Method	Frequency 1 (rarely) to 5 (frequently)	Effectiveness 1 (not effective) to 5 (very effective)	Feelings and Outcomes

Enhancing Resilience Through Distress Tolerance

In this section, we'll cover distress tolerance skills that will help you manage the effects of narcissistic abuse and gaslighting effectively when you find yourself triggered.

> When you are using distress tolerance skills, it can be beneficial to rate your distress level before and after using a scale from 0 (no distress) to 10 (the most distress ever). This will help you to identify how your distress level has decreased and help you recognize when you may need to use more than one distress tolerance skill to bring your distress level down. The goal with using these skills is not to bring your distress level to 0 every time, but to experience a decrease in the intensity of the emotion and feel an increase in your present-moment awareness.

Accessing distress tolerance skills can be challenging when you're dysregulated due to trauma triggers, but even when your system is overwhelmed, you have portable coping skills readily available. Using your breath and senses, you can ground yourself in the present moment, effectively redirecting your attention away from distressing thoughts and memories related to your experiences with narcissistic abuse and gaslighting; breath and senses skills promote emotional regulation, enhance decision making, and reaffirm your connection to the present moment. With these skills, you can effectively manage your response to triggers and regain a sense of control and safety in the aftermath of the trauma related to the narcissistic abuse you suffered.

The Breath

When you are confronted with triggers that evoke intense emotional and physiological responses related to the abuse you've suffered, intentional breath awareness can be a calming anchor. The two breathing techniques we'll cover are highly effective at activating the body's parasympathetic nervous system, reducing the intensity of the stress response, promoting relaxation, reducing stress and anxiety, enhancing self-control, helping you manage intense emotions, and reconnecting you with your physical self in the present moment. (More breathing exercises can be found on the Breathe and Be Well worksheet, available for download with this book's other free tools at https://www.newharbinger.com/52892.)

4-7-8 BREATHING

1. **Sit or lie down in a comfortable position:** You can have your eyes open or closed depending on your comfort level. Throughout the activity, stay focused on the sensation of your breath.

2. **Inhale for a count of 4:** Take a slow, deep breath through your nose, counting silently to 4 as you inhale. Feel the breath filling your lungs.

3. **Hold your breath for a count of 7:** Focus on the stillness and the sensation of the breath within you.

4. **Exhale for a count of 8:** Slowly and completely exhale through your mouth, counting silently to 8. Empty your lungs completely.

5. **Repeat this cycle for several breaths,** ideally for a few minutes.

BOX BREATHING

1. **Sit or lie down in a comfortable position:** You can have your eyes open or closed depending on your comfort level. Throughout the activity, stay focused on the sensation of your breath; envision tracing the outline of an imaginary box in your mind to enhance your mindfulness and deepen your connection with the present moment.

2. **Inhale for a count of 4:** Take a slow, deep breath in through your nose, counting silently to 4 as you inhale.

3. **Hold your breath for a count of 4:** During this pause, focus on the stillness and the sensation of the breath within you.

4. **Exhale for a count of 4:** Exhale slowly and completely through your mouth, counting silently to 4. Release all the air from your lungs.

5. **Hold for a count of 4:** Maintain stillness and focus.

6. **Repeat this cycle for several breaths.**

Using Your Senses

Perpetrators of narcissistic abuse and gaslighting try to manipulate your perception of reality to create confusion and self-doubt. Engaging your senses through tactile, visual, auditory, or olfactory stimuli provides immediate sensory input that grounds you in the present moment, anchoring yourself to what is real and tangible and reducing the impact of the perpetrator's manipulation. Using your senses helps pull your attention away from trauma triggers.

ACTIVATING YOUR SENSES WITH 5-4-3-2-1

List the following, either in your head or out loud:

- **5 things you can see:** Begin by looking around your immediate environment and identify 5 things you can see. They can be anything in your surroundings, such as a chair, a book, a plant, or a piece of artwork.

- **4 things you can touch:** Shift your focus to the sense of touch. Identify 4 things you can physically touch or feel. For example, the texture of your clothing or the smooth surface of a table.

- **3 things you can hear:** Pay attention to the sounds in your environment and pick out 3 things you can hear. These sounds could be in the background, like the hum of appliances or distant traffic, or specific, like a bird singing or the ticking of a clock.

- **2 things you can smell:** Focus on your sense of smell and identify 2 scents in your surroundings. They could include the smell of a nearby flower or the fragrance of your soap or lotion.

- **1 thing you can taste:** Last, explore your sense of taste by identifying 1 thing you can taste now. It might be the lingering flavor of a recent meal or the freshness of a mint.

CREATE A GROUNDING BOX

Creating a physical grounding box is a hands-on way to identify soothing and anchoring objects that you can use to ground yourself in the present moment—by activating your senses—when you are triggered, or during other difficult times.

Step 1. Choose a container: Select a physical box or other container. It can be a small wooden box, a decorative tin, or any container that feels meaningful or comforting. It needs to be sturdy and capable of holding all the objects you'll choose to put in it.

Step 2. Select an item to represent each of your five senses:

- Sight (visual)—include an object that brings you visual comfort, such as a colorful trinket or an image of a calming landscape.

- Touch (tactile)—include something you can touch and feel when needed, such as a smooth stone or a textured fidget item.

- Hearing (auditory)—include an item with soothing sounds, such as a small chime or a list of calming music that you can listen to.

- Smell (olfactory)—include something with a pleasant scent, such as a candle or essential oil–infused cotton balls.

- Taste (gustatory)—include something small that appeals to your taste buds and brings you a sense of comfort, such as a specific treat or a tea bag.

Step 3. Arrange your grounding box: Place each item inside your chosen container. You can organize them in a way that feels visually pleasing or that makes them easily accessible.

Step 4. Utilize the grounding box in distressing moments: When you feel overwhelmed, distressed, or triggered, you can take out your grounding box and consciously be present with each item.

GROUNDING THROUGH COUNTING

Counting can help you manage intense emotions by redirecting your focus to a simple and structured task. It provides a mental distraction from distressing thoughts and allows you to decrease rumination. Counting can also serve as a cognitive grounding tool, prompting you to focus on the present moment to avoid manipulation.

1. **Choose a counting pattern:**

   Counting up—start from a specific number and count up by 3s.

   Counting down—start with a high number and count down by 3s.

   Count using prime numbers—count up or down using numbers divisible only by 1 and themselves.

2. **Begin counting:** Start counting using your chosen pattern.

3. **Maintain focus:** As you count, concentrate solely on the act of counting.

4. **Interrupt intrusive thoughts:** If you become overwhelmed by distressing thoughts or memories related to narcissistic abuse and gaslighting, gently bring your focus back to the counting.

5. **Continue as needed:** You can continue counting for as long as you need to manage ongoing distress.

USING COOL TEMPERATURES

Touching something that has a cool temperature is a sensory grounding technique that can help you shift your attention away from trauma-related triggers, memories, or thoughts. Not only does this skill help you manage the aftereffects of narcissistic abuse and gaslighting, it can also help you manage intrusive thoughts, help you regulate your emotional responses, and provide a physical anchor for times when you feel disconnected and overwhelmed.

1. **Identify a cool sensation:** Find something that provides a cold sensation. It could be a glass of cold water or an ice pack. You could also step outside on a chilly day.

2. **Engage your senses:** Focus your attention on the cool sensation.

3. **Breathe mindfully:** As you experience the cool sensation, take slow, deep breaths. Stay focused on the sensation of coolness and notice your breathing.

4. **Stay present:** Keep your focus on the cool sensation and your breath. If your mind starts to wander to distressing thoughts or memories, gently bring your attention back to the sensation of coolness.

Here are some ideas for practicing:

- Splashing cold water on your face

- Applying a cold compress to your forehead or the back of your neck

- Sipping an ice-cold drink

- Holding on to ice or a frozen orange

- Taking a walk in the cold

DISTRACTING WITH DISTRACT

When you're triggered or feel emotionally dysregulated, it can be difficult to identify what skills you should use. Distracting with DISTRACT provides you with an easy-to-remember acronym that will remind you of various skills available to help you shift your attention away from distressing triggers related to narcissistic abuse and gaslighting. This skill aims to bring your focus to the present moment, offering a powerful way to regain control and maintain emotional balance in the face of manipulative tactics and psychological distress.

DISTRACT stands for:

D: Do something! When you recognize you're triggered, engaging in grounding activities is important.

I: Imagine a container and put all the distressing emotions, thoughts, and memories into it so you can bring your awareness to the present moment.

S: Step outside into nature. Go for a walk or a run, or just step outside and breathe the fresh air.

T: Turn on music! Listen to your favorite songs.

R: Reach out to a friend or family member for support or to be distracted from your current situation.

A: Allow yourself to rest. Take a nap or take a break from technology for a while.

C: Count the things around you, bringing your attention to the present moment.

T: Take five deep breaths, breathing out longer than you are breathing in, focusing on the sensation of the breath in this present moment.

Using Your Skills

One of the best things about distress tolerance skills is that there are so many at your disposal. If one doesn't work, you can try another! We went over quite a few in this chapter, but there are so many more; see the list Expanded Grounding and Distraction Techniques for Distress Tolerance, available for download with this book's free tools at https://www.newhar binger.com/52892.

The key to having success with distress tolerance skills is to practice them ahead of time, when you're not dysregulated. Familiarizing yourself with the skills this way will help make it easier for you to access them in times of need. Don't forget that you always carry with you portable skills in the form of your breath and senses; use these skills in times of need to reclaim your inner calm.

Moving Forward on the Path Toward Healing and Recovery

Distress tolerance skills are crucial to your healing and recovery from narcissistic abuse. By learning how to regulate intense emotions, self-soothe, and stay present even during emotionally distressing times, you can gradually regain control over your life. As you integrate these skills into your life to manage trauma-related triggers, your world will stop feeling like it's spinning out of control, and you'll be able to rebuild your self-esteem and reclaim your sense of self-worth. Remember, healing and recovering from narcissistic abuse and gaslighting is a journey, and every step you take toward integrating these skills into your daily life is moving you closer to reclaiming yourself.

CHAPTER 9

Reevaluating Your Thoughts

One of the most profound and pervasive impacts of narcissistic abuse is the effect it has on your thoughts about and perceptions of yourself, others, and the world around you. Tactics of manipulation, gaslighting, and devaluation lead to cognitive distortions, reinforcing negative core beliefs and intrusive thinking, both of which are dysregulating. You may know that cognitive distortions and intrusive thoughts are common trauma reactions, but this knowledge alone isn't enough to counteract the emotional impact of manipulation, gaslighting, and devaluation.

The repetitive and relentless nature of narcissistic abuse, in the form of negative comments, slowly chips away at your sense of self-worth, causing you to completely deny the truth of your perceptions, leading to a decrease in self-trust. It's as if narcissistic abuse and gaslighting rewire your brain, embedding negative messages so deeply that you lose your ability to challenge them, and over time you come to believe they're true. You begin to think that something is wrong with you, that you are the problem.

That is certainly not true, but challenging, shifting, and changing your thoughts about yourself, others, and the world around you after experiencing narcissistic abuse and gaslighting isn't easy. Changing your thinking patterns requires a continuous and conscious effort; you must identify, acknowledge, and counteract intrusive and negative thoughts relentlessly. The skills in this chapter can help you do just that. By identifying cognitive distortions and developing skills to manage intrusive thoughts, you can regain control over your thoughts.

Narcissistic Abuse While Dating: Alex's Story

Alex felt like their relationship with Jordan had begun like a fairy tale. They fell deeply in love with Jordan. A year into the relationship, Alex began to notice a shift in Jordan's behavior. There were subtle belittling comments about their appearance and put-downs about the way they did everyday tasks. Jordan's words began to chip away at Alex's self-esteem. They felt stuck, never feeling good enough or worthy but still seeking Jordan's support, approval, and validation anyway.

The manipulation extended beyond words. Jordan frequently gaslit Alex, denying that certain conversations had taken place, conveniently forgetting promises made, and shifting blame onto Alex for any problems in the relationship. This constant distortion of reality left Alex confused and isolated, and they began to lose trust in their perceptions, thoughts, and memories. Constantly second-guessing themselves and their judgments, they started worrying that their faults would cause Jordan to leave them; they spent countless hours ruminating on worst-case scenarios. Jordan exploited this fear of abandonment, keeping Alex fearful and dependent.

Narcissistic Abuse, Gaslighting, and Your Thoughts

Perpetrators of narcissistic abuse use various tactics to create a world in which you don't trust your thoughts and perceptions, as Jordan did with Alex. They will gaslight you, engage others in gaslighting you, use blame-shifting, manipulate, and project their negative emotions and qualities onto you. Consequently, you develop automatic negative thoughts that reinforce the various cognitive distortions the perpetrator of narcissistic abuse and gaslighting has cultivated.

Automatic negative thoughts and distortions are often painful and trigger emotional distress. Our goal in this chapter is to not only identify your negative thoughts and distortions, but also to begin to challenge them, shifting your thinking, decreasing your emotional pain, and kicking the internalized voice of the perpetrator out of your head.

Automatic Negative Thoughts

Automatic negative thoughts occur quickly in response to painful situations or triggers. They come into your mind involuntarily, interrupting your thinking, and are often accompanied by distressing emotions such as guilt, anger, shame, self-blame, and sadness. After experiencing narcissistic abuse and gaslighting, you may experience automatic negative thoughts relating to your self-worth and the validity of your feelings and find that you doubt your emotions, memories, and perceptions. You may find that you struggle with self-blame and critical thoughts, ruminate and obsess about the past, and worry about your future, fear that you'll always feel damaged and that the lingering effects of the abuse will hold you back from living the life you desire.

The following list includes some of the most common automatic thoughts that survivors of narcissistic abuse report experiencing. Place a checkmark next to the thoughts you've had before. This is not an exhaustive list, and there are blank spaces for you to write in any other automatic thoughts you're currently struggling with or have struggled with in the past.

- ☐ I'm always wrong.
- ☐ I can't do anything right.
- ☐ It's my fault.
- ☐ I'm the problem.
- ☐ I'm just being too sensitive.
- ☐ No one else will ever love me.
- ☐ I will be alone forever.
- ☐ I must have done something to upset them.
- ☐ I can't make any mistakes.
- ☐ It wasn't that bad.
- ☐ I'm not good enough.
- ☐ I'll never be happy.
- ☐ I can't escape this.

☐ I can't trust anyone.

☐ I must be crazy.

☐ I am broken.

☐ _____

☐ _____

These automatic thoughts are a natural response to the abuse you've endured, and you are not alone in having them. Most importantly, these thoughts do not define you. Even though identifying and acknowledging these thoughts is painful, by doing so you are taking an important step toward healing and recovering from narcissistic abuse and gaslighting.

Cognitive Distortions

Cognitive distortions are irrational patterns of thinking that cause you to interpret situations in ways that reinforce negative beliefs you have about yourself, your values, other people, and the world around you. The various tactics of narcissistic abuse you've experienced can cause you to develop such distorted beliefs. Accepting these distortions as truths leads to intense emotions, distress, and a sense of helplessness. Your belief in cognitive distortions, which has been reinforced repeatedly by the perpetrator of narcissistic abuse, can lead to a pervasive sense of hopelessness and the belief that things will never change.

The first step to challenging cognitive distortions is to identify those you're having. Below is a list of cognitive distortions survivors of narcissistic abuse and gaslighting, such as yourself, commonly experience. Put a checkmark next to those you've experienced.

☐ Catastrophizing: believing the worst will always happen

☐ Overgeneralization: applying past trauma to all future situations

☐ All-or-nothing thinking: seeing things as all good or all bad

☐ Personalization: blaming oneself for traumatic events

☐ Discounting the positive: ignoring or downplaying positive experiences

☐ Mind reading: assuming others are judging you negatively

☐ Emotional reasoning: believing your feelings always reflect reality

- [ ] Should-statements: setting unrealistic expectations

- [ ] Labeling: using harsh labels to describe yourself

- [ ] Selective abstraction: focusing on one negative detail; ignoring the bigger picture

When you believe in a cognitive distortion and accept it as the truth, it can profoundly affect your sense of self and mental well-being. Identifying cognitive distortions helps you become more aware of your thought patterns so that you can begin to dismantle them by challenging and reframing them. Doing so will help you to regulate your emotions more effectively and reduce the intensity of your negative feelings.

From Doubt to Clarity: Reclaiming Your Thoughts After Gaslighting

Healing from the effects of narcissistic abuse and gaslighting takes time. Often, it takes much longer than you would have hoped. It feels like negative and distressing automatic thoughts enter your brain so fast that you can't control or manage them. We're going to look at skills you can use to begin to regain control of your thoughts and challenge the perceptions of the perpetrator you may have internalized.

SHIFTING YOUR THOUGHTS BY RECORDING YOUR ABUSE-TRIGGERED AUTOMATIC THOUGHTS

Automatic thoughts and cognitive distortions develop in narcissistically abusive relationships due to manipulation, control, gaslighting, and other psychological tactics of abuse used by the perpetrator to minimize, confuse, and instill fear in you. The following modified thought record, tailored to focus on your experiences with narcissistic abuse, is a highly effective and efficient tool for identifying how your automatic thoughts and cognitive distortions lead to intense emotional distress. Not only is it a valuable tool for increasing your awareness of your negative thoughts and distortions that developed as a result of the abuse you experienced, it's also great for validating your emotions and supporting your recovery from narcissistic abuse and gaslighting. Use the example from Alex's relationship with Jordan to guide you in completing your own Narcissistic Abuse Automatic Thoughts Record, available for download with this book's free tools at https://www.newharbinger.com/52892.

NARCISSISTIC ABUSE AUTOMATIC THOUGHTS RECORD

Triggering situation: Describe the specific situation or trigger that led to your abuse-triggered automatic thought. Be as detailed as possible.	Recognizing the abuse-triggered automatic thought: Write down the thought that popped into your mind in response to the situation. Try to capture the exact wording of your thought.	Identifying the cognitive distortion: Identify the cognitive distortion(s) associated with your automatic thought. Cognitive distortions are irrational or biased ways of thinking that can lead to negative emotions.	Rating your emotion response (0–10): Rate the intensity of the emotions you felt in response to your automatic thought using a scale from 0 (no emotion) to 10 (extremely intense emotion). Be honest about your feelings.	Evidence to refute the abuse-triggered automatic thought: List evidence contradicting or challenging your automatic thought. Are there alternative interpretations or facts you may have overlooked?	Identifying your resilient thought: Generate a more balanced and rational thought based on your gathered evidence. It should be more accurate and less biased and empower you to maintain your mental well-being and navigate the challenges of healing from narcissistic abuse with a balanced and compassionate mindset.	Rerating your emotions (0–10): After considering the more balanced thought, rate the intensity of your emotions again using the same 0 (no emotion) to 10 (extremely intense emotion) scale. Note any changes in your emotional response. Make note of and rate any new emotional responses that you become aware of.
I brought up a past conversation, and Jordan denied it ever happened.	I must be losing my mind. I can't trust my own memory.	Emotional reasoning and personalization	9: Intensely anxious 8: Confused	I have a record of the conversation saved in my messages. I have always had a reliable memory in other aspects of life, and no one else in my life has ever reported concerns about me forgetting things.	I have evidence of the conversation. It's okay to trust my memory and judgment. Jordan's denial doesn't define my reality.	3: Significantly less anxious 6: Feeling more confident in my personal judgment

Challenging Intrusive Thoughts

Intrusive thoughts are distressing and disturbing thoughts that involuntarily enter your mind. These thoughts can focus on experiences you've had with narcissistic abuse and gaslighting or negative perceptions or beliefs you've formed about yourself due to the abuse. They can cause you to replay past incidents of abuse, obsess over the perpetrator's behavior, or even entertain thoughts of revenge. You may experience reoccurring thoughts centered on self-doubt, guilt, shame, and worthlessness, leading to persistent negative emotions. You can interrupt these intrusive thoughts using the STOP intrusive thoughts skill (adapted from Linehan 2015), which can reduce your emotional distress and prevent rumination, and begin to take back control of your thoughts.

EXERCISE: STOP Intrusive Thoughts

S—Suspend:

- When you notice intrusive or negative thoughts, the first step is to interrupt them.

- Take a moment to pause and acknowledge without judgment that these thoughts are present. This will allow you the space necessary to process them.

T—Take in:

- After acknowledging the intrusive thoughts, take in a few deep breaths to ground yourself in the present moment.

- Choose a breathing technique that works best for you, or use one of the breathing techniques offered in the last chapter or on the Breathe and Be Well worksheet, available for download with this book's other free tools at https://www.new harbinger.com/52892.

O—Open your mind and reflect:

- With a calm, centered, and open mind, just notice your thoughts and feelings related to the intrusive or negative thoughts.

- Reflect on what triggered these intrusive or negative thoughts and how they've affected you emotionally and physically.

- Ask yourself questions like, "Why do I feel this way?" and "What specific beliefs or assumptions drive these thoughts?"

P—Perspective:

- Consider different perspectives of the abuse-triggered intrusive thoughts. Try to view them from a broader, more objective standpoint.

- Ask yourself if there might be an alternative or more balanced thought that you haven't considered.

- Choose how you want to respond to the abuse-triggered intrusive or negative thoughts. This response may include using mindfulness, completing a Narcissistic Abuse Automatic Thoughts Record, or practicing self-care using the Mindful Me: Self-Care Inspiration Worksheet, both available for download with this book's free tools at https://www.newharbinger.com/52892.

Moving Forward on the Path Toward Healing and Recovery

When learning the skills in this chapter, you may need to revisit them frequently to help manage distressing trauma-related thoughts. Over time, as you use techniques such as the Narcissistic Abuse Automatic Thoughts Record to challenge your thoughts and gain control of them, you will notice a positive shift in your thoughts and perceptions of yourself, people, and the world around you. This shift will present as an increase in feelings of self-worth, an improved sense of self-awareness, a sense of empowerment, and increased confidence in trusting your instincts.

Narcissistic abuse is repetitive. In such relationships, you regularly receive negative, hurtful, critical, and belittling messages from the perpetrator. Over time, you begin to believe in these messages and accept them as truths about who you are. These messages are false; they do not describe you or define you, but they can profoundly affect your mental health. The more you identify and challenge negative thoughts and cognitive distortions, the more you poke holes in their narratives. Becoming aware of negative thinking and distorted thought patterns is another step toward healing, recovery, and reclaiming your sense of autonomy.

CHAPTER 10

Restoring Who You Are and Moving Forward

Invisible wounds run the deepest, and those that come from surviving narcissistic abuse and gaslighting are no exception. No one asks to experience narcissistic abuse; more importantly, no one deserves to experience this form of abuse. While you can't erase what happened in the past, you can control what your healing and recovery journey looks like. For many survivors of narcissistic abuse and gaslighting, the idea of ever being able to move forward feels far-fetched. However, you *can* move forward, heal, rediscover yourself, regain a sense of security, and learn to trust others and yourself again.

The preceding chapters of this workbook focused on helping you cope with the effects of narcissistic abuse and gaslighting as they are impacting you in the present moment. The skills you've developed have addressed how this abuse has impacted your relationships, your emotions, and your thoughts. This chapter is different; its content is meant to support your healing and recovery journey that will extend far beyond the pages of this workbook. The skills in this chapter are not about the past but your future.

As we near the end of the book, it's essential to acknowledge that no amount of therapy or number of workbooks can erase the experiences you've had with narcissistic abuse and gaslighting. Therapy and workbooks alone can't heal you. The variable that will make those changes is you.

Narcissistic Abuse, Gaslighting, and Healing: Your Story

As we journeyed together through this workbook, you read about the narcissistic abuse and gaslighting that others have experienced in all types of relationships. For this chapter, the story is yours. It's your time to reflect on your healing and recovery process, and on the future. The following space is for you to reflect on how far you've come, and on what you're looking forward to on the journey ahead with your newfound sense of autonomy, empowerment, wholeness, and self-love.

REFLECTING ON YOUR JOURNEY

Feel free to write whatever comes to mind, or use the prompts below to guide you, or both.

- How have I grown emotionally and mentally since I began my healing journey?

- What were the most significant turning points in my recovery from narcissistic abuse and gaslighting?

- Reflect on a moment when I felt particularly empowered in my healing process. What led to that feeling of strength?

- How has my understanding of self-love evolved in this recovery process?

_____

_____

_____

_____

_____

_____

_____

_____

_____

_____

_____

_____

_____

_____

Thriving Beyond Narcissistic Abuse and Gaslighting

"Thriving" describes a state of flourishing, significant growth, and well-being in all aspects of one's life, including physical, mental, and emotional health; career success; personal relationships; and sense of purpose and satisfaction. When we are thriving, we've moved beyond surviving and can pursue our goals, experience fulfillment, and live our best life. Thriving is your next step on your journey of healing and recovery from narcissistic abuse.

You may have thought you'd never make it to this place in your journey. In times when life is dark and both your internal and external worlds have been shattered, it's hard even to acknowledge that a state of being such as thriving exists. As such, we must take a moment to pause here and allow ourselves to bask in this state of thriving. The following list of affirmations can remind you of your ongoing growth, resilience, and self-worth. Use these reminders daily, or come back to them as needed, to remind yourself of your progress.

As you read through this list, I encourage you to move slowly and allow yourself time to sit with each affirmation, recognizing the growth, strength, and braveness you possess. First, read the affirmation, then say it out loud twice. It may even help to look in the mirror as you recite these affirmations.

- I am grateful for the strength I have within.

- I embrace my bright future.

- I have overcome adversity, and I will keep growing stronger.

- I am surrounded by positivity.

- I trust in my ability to navigate life's challenges.

- I celebrate my accomplishments.

- I am proud of the person I have become and love myself.

- I can radically accept my past, and I choose to focus on the present and future.

- I deserve all the happiness and success that come my way.

- I am an inspiration to others who may be healing.

- I am thriving.

Thriving Every Day

Healing from narcissistic abuse and gaslighting is a challenging journey filled with ups and downs that test you to your core, but ultimately it led you to where you are now—a space in which you can thrive. Acknowledging how you are thriving is essential for your emotional and mental well-being. Doing so is empowering, is validating, and provides hope. If you're faced with challenges in the future, acknowledging how you're thriving can remind you of just how far you've come.

Place a checkmark next to the ways you're thriving. In the blank spaces, write in the ways you are thriving that aren't included on the list.

Empowerment Checklist: How You're Thriving

- ☐ Built healthier relationships

- ☐ Embraced self-love

- ☐ Achieved a career goal

- ☐ Developed boundaries

- ☐ Regained independence

- ☐ Enhanced my self-esteem

- ☐ Improved my communication skills

☐ Rediscovered hobbies and interests

☐ Overcame fears

☐ Adopted a healthier lifestyle

☐ Developed financial independence

☐ Strengthened my support system

☐ Reclaimed my identity

☐ Developed a sense of autonomy

☐ Rebuilt trust in myself

☐ I know I am thriving because I have _____.

☐ I know I am thriving because I have _____.

☐ I know I am thriving because I have: _____.

Coping with Difficult Situations Ahead

Even though you're nearing the end of the workbook and have developed a host of new skills, there still may be times when you're faced with distressing situations or trauma triggers. The most effective way to work through these situations and triggers and continue to thrive is to prepare yourself to the best of your abilities. The following skill can help you do just that. It walks you through steps that help you imagine what it will be like to cope with a challenging situation or trigger related to narcissistic abuse and gaslighting. Being prepared will help increase your self-confidence and the likelihood that you'll respond in a way that makes you proud. Follow the steps below and rehearse how you can effectively cope with a trauma trigger or difficult situation.

THRIVE THROUGH TRIGGERS: Advanced Coping Strategies for Narcissistic Challenges

1. **Identify a potential trigger or difficult situation in which you'd need to apply this skill:** It could be related to your emotions, relationships, work, or any other aspect of your life.

2. **Describe the situation or trigger:** Write down a detailed description, including what is likely to happen, the emotions that may be triggered, and your typical reactions to such situations or triggers. Be as specific as possible.

3. **Prepare for emotional responses:** Consider how you think you will feel. Are you likely to feel angry, anxious, sad, or overwhelmed? Recognize and acknowledge these emotions.

4. **Identify coping strategies:** Now that you have a clear understanding of the situation or trigger and your emotional responses, plan which specific coping strategies you can use to manage the distress. These strategies should be healthy and effective ways to regulate emotions and behavior.

5. **Self-soothing techniques:** Identify activities or practices you can use to help you calm down and relax, such as deep breathing, mindfulness, or a grounding box (see chapter 8).

6. **Problem solving:** If the situation or trigger involves a problem that can be solved, brainstorm possible solutions and plan your actions accordingly.

7. **Assertiveness:** If the situation or trigger involves interpersonal conflict, plan how you will assertively communicate your needs and boundaries while maintaining respect for yourself and others.

8. **Distract yourself:** Have a list of distractions or activities that can shift your focus away from the distressing situation or trigger, if needed.

9. **Rehearse:** Practice implementing your coping strategies in your mind or through role-playing with a friend or family member. Visualization and rehearsal will make it easier to apply these strategies when the actual situation or trigger arises.

10. **Implement the plan:** When encountering a distressing situation or trigger, use the coping strategies you've planned and practiced.

If going forward you're worried about specific triggers or challenging situations related to your experiences with abuse, it will be helpful to practice this skill, to help you decrease your distress and anxiety around potential future triggers and situations, as well as to help you rebuild your sense of self-esteem.

Rediscovering Your Passions

Reconnecting with your passions, such as interests and hobbies, is just as crucial for your healing and recovery as developing skills that help you cope with potential triggers and distressing situations. Rediscovering and engaging your passions helps you to reclaim your identity, allowing you to connect with the real you without the influence of narcissistic abuse and gaslighting. When you engage in your passions, your self-esteem is boosted and you have a sense of accomplishment and empowerment. Let's do an exercise to help you explore what you might be passionate about.

EXERCISE: Discovering Your Passions— Hobbies and Interests Exploration

1. **Setting the mood:** Find a quiet and comfortable space where you won't be disturbed.

2. **Reflect on your past interests:** For five to ten minutes, reflect on the interests and hobbies you had before the abusive relationship. What activities did you enjoy doing in the past? Write down as many as you can remember.

_____

_____

_____

_____

_____

_____

_____

3. **Identify your current interests:** Write down a list of activities or interests that spark your curiosity or excitement.

_____

_____

_____

_____

_____

_____

4. **Set goals and priorities:** Based on your reflections, set goals for incorporating these interests into your life. What steps can you take to prioritize these interests to create a more fulfilling daily routine? How will you feel when you explore these interests? What will you gain from engaging in these interests?

_____

_____

_____

_____

_____

_____

Take each goal and break it down into two or three action steps, making sure to note when you will start engaging in these interests.

_____

_____

_____

_____

_____

_____

_____

_____

5. **Reflect:** Take a moment to reflect on the importance of rediscovering your passions and focusing on the positive aspects of your life. Allow yourself to acknowledge how you will feel once you engage in your interests, and bask in that feeling for several minutes, picturing yourself enjoying the activities you've identified.

Building Healthy Foundations

The idea of being in future relationships, no matter the type, may be frightening. It's important to remember that you can set healthy and effective boundaries for yourself. Remember, you are allowed to set boundaries and maintain them. Below, you'll prepare yourself for those future relationships by identifying what you want, need, and desire from them.

EXERCISE: Exploring Relationship Needs and Desires

This exercise will help you identify what you're looking for in relationships. In the spaces below, list your essential needs, additional wants, and long-term desires for each type of relationship. When identifying your needs, wants, and desires, don't forget to keep your values in mind.

Friendships

I need _____

_____.

I want _____

_____.

I desire _____

_____.

Romantic Relationships

I need _____

_____.

I want _____

_____.

I desire _____

_____.

Family Relationships

I need _____

_____.

I want _____

_____.

I desire _____

_____.

Work Relationships

I need _____

_____.

I want _____

_____.

I desire _____

_____.

Acquaintances

I need _____

_____.

I want _____

_____.

I desire _____

_____.

Other Types of Relationships

I need _____

_____.

I want _____

_____.

I desire _____

_____.

Renewal and Resilience: Embracing Gratitude

Gratitude is a powerful component in your journey of healing from narcissistic abuse and gaslighting. When you practice gratitude, you can shift away from the negative aspects of your past and instead focus on the positive aspects of your life. Practicing gratitude allows you to tap into positive emotions like joy, hope, and love. Keeping a gratitude journal can enhance your resilience, helping you see your inner strength and self-confidence.

EXERCISE: Gratitude Journal

Here are some tips for keeping a gratitude journal.

- **Choose a journal:** Select a notebook, journal, or digital journaling app that you find visually appealing and enjoyable to write in.

- **Set a regular time:** Pick a specific time to write in your gratitude journal each day. Consistency is key.

- **Write three things:** Each day, write down at least three things you are grateful for.

- **Reflect on the positive:** Take a moment to reflect on the positive aspects of your life, no matter how small or insignificant they may seem.

- **Express why you're grateful:** Briefly explain why you're grateful for each item. What impact did it have on your day, or has it had on your life? How does it make you feel?

- **Embrace challenges:** Sometimes challenges and difficulties can teach us valuable lessons. Consider writing about something you're grateful for even in challenging situations.

- **Avoid repetition:** While repeating things you're grateful for is okay, try to find new things each day to be grateful for.

- **Stay consistent:** Make gratitude journaling a daily habit. The more you do it, the more you'll notice positive changes in your mindset.

You can use these tips to complete the gratitude journal each day, or if you'd rather, you can use some of the following prompts to serve as your focus for your practice of gratitude. Choose the ones that resonate the most with you when it comes to gratitude.

Gratitude Prompts

- What made you smile today, and why?

- Describe a small act of kindness you witnessed or received today.

- What aspect of your health are you grateful for today?

- Write about a person in your life who has positively impacted you recently.

- What is something you take for granted that you are thankful for today?

- Reflect on a challenging situation or setback. What did you learn from it that you can be grateful for?

- Write about a place or environment that makes you feel at peace or happy.

Reflecting on Your Past, Embracing Your Present, and Envisioning Your Future

Turning around and looking down the mountain path to see how far you've climbed is as important as looking ahead to where you're going. You can use knowledge and information from your past and present to help you identify how you will continue to thrive in the future in all aspects of your life.

EXERCISE: Reclaiming Your Narrative

Reflect on your past: Take some time to reflect on your past experiences with narcissistic abuse and gaslighting. Write down the key moments, emotions, and challenges you faced. Frame these experiences in terms of what you've learned and how they've shaped you into a stronger person. Here are some questions for you to reflect on while doing this:

What were the most challenging moments during the abuse?

_____

_____

_____

_____

_____

_____

_____

_____

How have these experiences helped you grow and become more resilient?

_____

_____

_____

_____

_____

_____

_____

What strengths did you develop as a result of overcoming these challenges?

_____

_____

_____

_____

_____

_____

_____

Embrace your present: Shift your focus to your current situation. Write about your feelings, your healing progress, and the positive changes you've made in your life since you were able to identify that you were experiencing narcissistic abuse. Consider these questions for reflection:

- How do you feel right now compared to when you were in the abusive relationship?

- What self-care practices have you incorporated into your daily routine?

- What are some recent achievements you've made or milestones you've marked in your healing journey?

_____

_____

_____

_____

_____

_____

_____

_____

_____

_____

Envision your future: Now look ahead. Imagine a future in which you're living your best, most fulfilling life. Write down your goals, dreams, and aspirations. Be as specific as possible and frame them in a positive light. Reflect on these questions:

- What are your short-term and long-term goals for your life and well-being?

- How do you see yourself thriving in the future?

- What positive changes would you like to make in your relationships, career, or personal development?

_____

_____

_____

_____

_____

_____

_____

_____

_____

Sometimes we are so ready to move on from our past that we forget to stop and reflect on how far we've come. Taking time to reflect on your past not only enables you to acknowledge and recognize that the pain you experienced was real, it allows you to remember the significant challenges you've overcome. When you reflect on the present moment, you make space to connect with your newfound sense of self-trust. When you pause and look forward, you can create a sense of hope and purpose, setting goals that align with your reestablished sense of self and self-worth.

Celebrating Your Success

You have done it! You are at the end of the workbook, basking in your sense of self-worth, love, and trust. The journey may not have been easy, but here you are! At the end of chapter 1, you identified several goals for healing and recovery. In the spaces below, transcribe these goals and revisit and reflect on them using the additional prompts. This process will allow you to recognize the progress you've made.

My goal for healing and recovery was:

_____

_____

I achieved my goal by

_____

_____

Because I achieved my goal I feel

_____

_____

My goal for healing and recovery was:

_____

_____

I achieved my goal by

_____

_____

Because I achieved my goal I feel

_____

_____

My goal for healing and recovery was:

_____

_____

I achieved my goal by

_____

_____

Because I achieved my goal I feel

_____

_____

Moving Forward on the Path Toward Healing and Recovery

Healing from narcissistic abuse and gaslighting is not linear. It is a complex and challenging process of rediscovering your self-worth, reclaiming your identity and autonomy, and rebuilding your ability to trust yourself. As you move forward, the skills you've learned and resilience you've gained will guide you toward a future based on your goals, wants, and desires, grounded in your values.

Take the skills you've cultivated in this workbook, apply them to your everyday life, balance them with self-compassion, and continue to thrive.

I leave you with my hopes and desires for you:

May you be happy.
May you be well.
May you be safe.
May you be peaceful and at ease.

References

Arnsten, A., C. M. Mazure, and R. Sinha. 2012. "This Is Your Brain in Meltdown." *Scientific American* 306: 48–53. https://doi.org/10.1038/scientificamerican0412-48.

Bourne, E. J. 2020. *The Anxiety and Phobia Workbook*, 7th ed. Oakland, CA: New Harbinger Publications.

Bremner, J. D., and M. T. Wittbrodt. 2020. "Stress, the Brain, and Trauma Spectrum Disorders." *International Review of Neurobiology* 152: 1–22. https://doi.org/10.1016/bs.irn.2020.01.004.

Carey, B. 2011. "Expert on Mental Illness Reveals Her Own Fight." *New York Times*, June 23. https://www.nytimes.com/2011/06/23/health/23lives.html.

Kabat-Zinn, J. 1994. *Wherever You Go, There You Are: Mindfulness Meditation in Everyday Life*. New York: Hyperion.

Linehan, M. M. 2015. *Cognitive-Behavioral Treatment of Borderline Personality Disorder*. New York: Guilford Press.

Lovering, N. 2022. "Healing from Childhood Trauma: The Roles of Neuroplasticity and EMDR." PsychCentral, May 9. https://psychcentral.com/ptsd/the-roles-neuroplasticity-and-emdr-play-in-healing-from-childhood-trauma.

Neff, K. D. 2009. "The Role of Self-Compassion in Development: A Healthier Way to Relate to Oneself." *Human Development* 52: 211–214. https://doi.org/10.1159/000215071.

———. 2023. "Self-Compassion." https://self-compassion.org/the-three-elements-of-self-compassion-2.

Shepherd, L., and J. Wild. 2014. "Emotion Regulation, Physiological Arousal and PTSD Symptoms in Trauma-Exposed Individuals." *Journal of Behavior Therapy and Experimental Psychiatry* 45: 360–367. https://doi.org/10.1016/j.jbtep.2014.03.002.

Short, N. A., J. W. Boffa, K. Clancy, and N. B. Schmidt. 2018. "Effects of Emotion Regulation Strategy Use in Response to Stressors on PTSD Symptoms: An Ecological Momentary Assessment Study." *Journal of Affective Disorders* 230: 77–83. https://doi.org/10.1016/j.jad.2017.12.063.

Substance Abuse and Mental Health Services Administration (SAMHSA). 2022. "Trauma and Violence." https://www.samhsa.gov/trauma-violence.

Katelyn Baxter-Musser, LCSW, C-DBT, is a licensed clinical social worker, an eye movement desensitization and reprocessing (EMDR) consultant, and is dialectical behavior therapy (DBT)-certified through Evergreen Certifications. In addition to her private practice, she is a national presenter for PESI, having trained thousands of mental health professionals on DBT, trauma, intimate partner violence, and mindfulness.

Foreword writer **Stephanie M. Kriesberg, PsyD**, has practiced clinical psychology for twenty-five years. She is trained in psychodynamic psychotherapy, cognitive behavioral therapy (CBT), and acceptance and commitment therapy (ACT), and is on the board of the New England Society of Clinical Hypnosis. She is author of *Adult Daughters of Narcissistic Mothers*.

MORE BOOKS from
NEW HARBINGER PUBLICATIONS

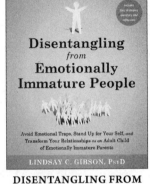
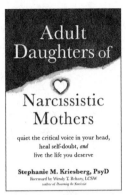

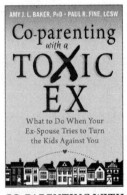
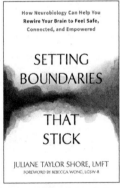

Did you know there are **free tools** you can download for this book?

Free tools are things like **worksheets, guided meditation exercises**, and **more** that will help you get the most out of your book.

You can download free tools for this book—whether you bought or borrowed it, in any format, from any source—from the New Harbinger website. All you need is a NewHarbinger.com account. Just use the URL provided in this book to view the free tools that are available for it. Then, click on the "download" button for the free tool you want, and follow the prompts that appear to log in to your NewHarbinger.com account and download the material.

You can also save the free tools for this book to your **Free Tools Library** so you can access them again anytime, just by logging in to your account! Just look for this button on the book's free tools page.

+ Save this to my free tools library

If you need help accessing or downloading free tools, visit **newharbinger.com/faq** or contact us at **customerservice@newharbinger.com**.